THE
SEVENTH
SYSTEM

STUART COHEN

THE
SEVENTH
SYSTEM

Harnessing the Power
of Your Emotional System

The Seventh System: *Harnessing the Power of Your Emotional System*

Website for book: www.SeventhSystem.net

ISBN-10 Number: 0-615408-67-2
ISBN-13/EAN 13 Number: 978-0-615408-67-5

Front Cover Photograph: ThinkStock.com
Interior Photographs: Stuart Cohen
Cover Design and Interior Layout: AuthorSupport.com

Dedicated to my mother, who taught me
by all that she told me, and my father,
who taught me by how he lived.

זכרונם לברכה

TABLE OF CONTENTS

Preface . . . . *ix*

Introduction . . . . *xi*

Chapter 1: A Healthy Emotional System 1

Chapter 2: Oneness: The Emotional System Seeks Connection . . .11

Chapter 3: Sorrowing: The Emotional System Seeks Resolution . .25

Chapter 4: The Art of the Truth .45

Chapter 5: Moving On 65

Chapter 6: The Circle of Emotions 73

Chapter 7: Feeling Follows Attention. 81

Chapter 8: Love. 91

Chapter 9: Social Connection 105

Chapter 10: Happiness 117

Chapter 11: Grief and Sadness 135

Chapter 12: Anger and Hatred 149

Chapter 13: Fear and Excitement 173

Chapter 14: Fluid Feelings 191

Chapter 15: Self Love 203

Bibliography *213*

PREFACE

Jet lag had me up before dawn that first day in Kathmandu in the Himalayan kingdom of Nepal. I found myself wandering through the ancient market area, watching the shopkeepers open their stalls as the morning light began to filter in.

I heard a scraping sound and looked down. A beggar boy with twisted legs dragged his body over to me. He looked up at me, put a pained expression on his face, and stretched out his hand for money. He was crusted with dirt, his clothes little more than rags.

No human life could have been further from mine in its earthly details. Yet as I looked into his eyes, something extraordinary happened. In an instant, all the differences between my western professional life and

> As I looked into his eyes, something extraordinary happened.

his tattered beggar existence fell away. I was overwhelmed by the feeling that he and I were somehow, on some level, the same.

That moment haunted me for years, and began to teach me about love.

INTRODUCTION

Humanity has evolved not just to survive but to thrive.

Something inside us impels us forward. It drives our thoughts and actions and guides us in how to live. It leads us to establish values. It moves us to form relationships for something greater than mere procreation. It inspires social evolution and the development of communities. It makes life worth living.

That "something" is emotion. Our feelings and emotions organize our lives from our earliest days until the end. They give life meaning.

Emotions are an essential and inseparable part of human life. All of us feel pretty much the same range of feelings. Each is triggered by specific life events and connected to our unique personal history.

All our emotions are interwoven with one another. As you come to comprehend how feelings arise and fit together,

> As you come to understand how feelings arise and fit together you will be able to make life more satisfying more of the time

you will learn to manage your feeling life more effectively. You will be able to steer yourself through difficult periods more easily and make life satisfying more of the time.

This is not a technical or scientific study. It is presented in ordinary language. Note that, for the purposes of this book, "emotions" are simply the feelings we feel; the two words "emotions" and "feelings" are used interchangeably.

CHAPTER 1

A Healthy Emotional System

We have all met people whose lives seem to sing. They take ups and downs in stride and maintain a generally positive outlook. Difficult feelings of sadness, anger and fear do not get them down for long. They seem glad to be alive.

What these people have in common is a healthy emotional system. They feel confident and relaxed most of the time and treat others with kindness. They set a wonderful example.

We can't change a lot of what happens around us in the normal course of living, and we can't avoid daily difficulties. But we *can* strengthen ourselves emotionally so that the hard times don't feel so bad and we don't get stuck in them. We can reorganize our feeling life to be more balanced, and more at peace.

What is Emotional Health?

A physically healthy body functions well most of the time. A cold virus knocks us down for a few days, and we recover. A cut finger heals. We expect our body's systems to naturally return us to a state of harmony and balance.

Emotional health works the same way. When we are emotionally healthy, our feelings, both pleasant and unpleasant, serve us. They help us make good decisions and move forward. Over the long term, emotional health allows us to manage the ebb and flow of our feelings.

Even those who are the healthiest emotionally don't feel good all the time. They sometimes endure painful, upsetting emotions just like everyone else. They feel the sting of loss and sadness every bit as deeply as the next person, but they recover more quickly. They suffer deeply in grief and may get furiously angry, but generally not often or for long. They do not carry grudges. Fear may grip them as sharply as it grips anyone, but they tend to find fewer reasons to be fearful.

> We can't change a lot of what happens to us on the outside. But we can strengthen ourselves emotionally so that the hard times don't feel so bad and we don't get stuck in them.

Emotionally healthy people are resilient. They keep their perspective when others might fall into despair. Unafraid of painful and powerful feelings, they are able to experience difficult emotions fully, and move on.

Emotionally less healthy people have a tougher time. They find it harder to recover from upsetting events. They may try to cling to happy feelings, hoping against hope to make a pleasant emotion stay, even after its time is past.

Emotionally *damaged* people may be unable to move through a full range of feelings at all. Their injured system of emotions, like a hurt shoulder, has a more restricted range. Bad feelings become a threat they strive to avoid. Good feelings are rare and serve more as a temporary relief than as a source of genuine pleasure.

> "In the last decade or so…, researchers have found that even more than IQ, your emotional awareness and abilities to handle feelings will determine your success and happiness in all walks of life."
> – JOHN GOTTMAN, in ***Raising an Emotionally Intelligent Child***

The Seven Systems

A *system* is an organized series of related parts that serve a purpose. All our body systems serve the same purpose: they keep us alive and well. Our six biological systems sustain life and health: the circulatory system regulates blood flow from the heart to every cell in the body, the digestive system extracts nutrients from food and excretes waste. We have a respiratory system, an endocrine system, a nervous system and an immune system. These physiological systems must be working right for us to survive. Should one of them fail, we would die.

We also have a seventh system, an emotional system. It governs our feelings. Like all the other systems, its job is to keep us stable, healthy and moving forward from morning to night, every day of our lives.

The emotional system is also different from the other six systems. Unlike our red blood cell count or lung capacity, emotions cannot be measured. While neurological research can indicate where specific emotional responses are seated in the brain and what chemicals activate them, the question of exactly how people feel emotions remains a mystery.

> The emotional system's job is to keep us stable, healthy and moving forward from morning to night, every day of our lives.

Stability and Equilibrium

Stability is the goal of all our bodily systems. When events happen that upset us emotionally, the emotional system quickly kicks in to restore equilibrium. It feels like something inside is calming us down, settling our fears and restoring our balance.

Sometimes, the automatic stabilizing effect of the emotional system can lead to other problems.

Patty was shocked numb when she learned that her brother's wife Teri had been diagnosed with an aggressive cancer and had only weeks to live. But when Teri died, Patty responded with supreme calm. "It's matter in transition," she said. "People die." While others grieved, Patty went about her business and offered support to other suffering relatives.

For months afterward, Patty spoke of Teri with hardly any emotion. Meanwhile, Patty's life stalled. She had little passion for work or play, and her relationships weakened as she calmly went about her work and looked after the needs of her family.

One day, three years after Teri's death, Patty was talking to her brother. "You know, I still miss Teri," she said. And the floodgates opened. Days of tears and deep grief followed as Patty released all the pent-up feelings of loss that had lain buried inside her.

Patty still speaks of Teri with a tear in her eye. In her other relationships, her life is much richer now.

Patty's emotional system stabilized her feelings in the short term. It took much longer to re-establish deeper emotional balance.

The Importance of Feelings

Feelings matter because they influence our every action and every choice. Feelings are our compass, our guide to how to live. We make important life decisions based on how we feel or expect to feel later on. An important part of the reason we do anything is to feel good.

"Having fun" means doing things that feel good right now. Our greatest accomplishments are considered great because of the feelings of pleasure and satisfaction that arise from them. Important relationships are all about the feelings of closeness that sustain them. Our goals and dreams would be empty without the strong positive emotion we expect them to generate. Even the arts succeed or fail on the basis of their emotional impact.

Sometimes, we seek immediate gratification. Other times, we pursue a greater good feeling later on. Eventually, everything we do that matters is tied to emotions. The pivotal events of life achieve their power because strong feelings etch them into memory for life, while less emotionally charged times are soon forgotten.

> The pivotal events of life achieve their power because strong feelings etch them into memory for life, while less emotionally charged times are soon forgotten.

Emotions help us make even ordinary decisions. Neurologist Antonio Damasio worked with a patient who had suffered brain damage that took away his emotions while leaving his rational mind intact. When asked when to make his next appointment, the man gave all sorts of reasons for which day and time might be best. But after a half hour of discussion, he was unable to make even such a simple decision as when to meet next.

Whether we realize it or not, we are always in pursuit of more satisfying and pleasurable emotions. Through relationships and activities, work and play, we constantly seek to create positive, good feelings of happiness, love and satisfaction. The drive for an emotional payoff frames all our choices.

Feelings are what make us human. How we feel determines the quality of our life experience.

Pursuit of Happiness

Can you be happy all the time? If you are in a terrific relationship, have an ideal job and plenty of money, would you be content all the time? Of course not. No emotion is permanent, just as no breath can be held for very long. Feelings shift continually. No matter your overall level of satisfaction, there will be moments when the bloom of happiness vanishes.

The chances are, however, that we can be happier. As we come to understand how our emotional system works,

> "Descartes' famous phrase, 'I think therefore I am' should really say, 'I feel, therefore I am.' "
> – ANTONIO DAMASIO, neurologist and author

we will learn how difficult and painful emotions contribute to our overall well-being. We will learn to let the down moments pass more quickly and bring ourselves back to more enjoyable emotions more easily.

THE MIND–BODY CONNECTION

The field of psychoneuroimmunology studies the influence of psychology and emotions on immune function and disease. Researchers have shown how an engaged and positive mental attitude can accelerate recovery from a variety of illnesses and even slow the spread of cancer.

An HMO in California offers free audiocassettes to guide patients on harnessing their imaginations to promote healing. They found that patients who used guided imagery tapes typically left the hospital earlier than others with similar conditions who did not.

Dr. Joan Borysenko, author and leading expert on the health connection between mind and body, says, "...taking care of the mind, which in turn generates our emotions, is the missing link when it comes to taking care of the body."

A seminal piece of mind-body research was Dr. Viktor Frankl's book, *Man's Search for Meaning*. Frankl's experience in a Nazi concentration camp showed him that prisoners whose lives had lost all meaning routinely died while those who were able to find meaning and purpose in one form or another were much more likely to survive.

Imagine a Journey

Our emotional life is like a drive along a mountain road. There are twists and turns, ups and downs. Sometimes we move forward easily; other times, we have to slow down for difficult terrain.

The road is full of blind spots and we don't know what awaits around the next corner. We do the best we can. Ahead may lie obstacles and perils or a spectacular new vista.

A healthy emotional system is like a dependable car on that mountain road. With it, we feel safe and confident, sure that we can negotiate every curve. Barring a catastrophe, we will manage just fine and won't crash or break down. We cruise through the beautiful times, tough out the hard climbs, and enjoy the wonders along the way.

> "A man who becomes conscious of the responsibility he bears toward a human being who affectionately waits for him, or to an unfinished work, will never be able to throw away his life. He knows the 'why' for his existence, and will be able to bear almost any 'how.'"
> – VICTOR FRANKL

Without a healthy emotional system, we are more likely to struggle. We might get stuck or break down. Everyone gets stuck sometimes. With a healthy, reliable emotional system we can recover from adversity and get ourselves back on the road to well-being.

Try this: Next time you're faced with an ordinary life choice—such as what restaurant to have dinner at or which movie to go see—experiment with trying to make the choice on the basis of reasons alone. Notice the tendency to want to check out your choice emotionally before you commit to it. Does it feel right? Emotions influence virtually everything we do.

Summary

- We have an emotional system that regulates our feeling life.
- Our emotional system's task is to keep us as emotionally balanced as possible for as much of the time as possible.
- Emotions are our barometer about how life is going. They guide us in making decisions.
- Feelings change continually: we can't hold onto any single emotional state.

CHAPTER 2

Oneness: The Emotional System Seeks *Connection*

Feeling connected, in tune, in touch, is what "feeling good" is all about. When our emotional system is working well, we find ourselves returning to a stable, positive feeling of harmony with the world around us, other people, and ourselves.

This powerful feeling is called *Oneness*. It is the personal, emotional experience of feeling connected, aligned and linked with people, our ideals and aspirations, or ourselves. *Oneness is the core experience at the heart of the emotional system.* It is also the root of all other emotions. The feeling of Oneness is our emotional source, where we come from and where we want to come back to when difficulties pull us away.

The job of the emotional system is to create and recreate feelings of Oneness. It does this naturally and automatically to keep us on balance and moving forward day after day and year after year.

Andrea was daydreaming while stuck in traffic. When the car in front of her stopped quickly, Andrea bumped into it, smashing a tail light. As soon as she had exchanged insurance information with the other driver, she pulled over and called her mother.

> "But what is happiness except the simple harmony between a man and the life he leads?"
> – ALBERT CAMUS, philosopher

Andrea's mother knew little about cars or insurance. But she had always been a source of stability and calm. Feeling shaky and upset about the accident, Andrea naturally sought to restore her emotional well-being by reconnecting with her mom. They only talked for a couple of minutes, but that was enough to settle Andrea's jangled nerves.

Andrea's emotional system had to respond to the upset of the accident. That meant pulling over and calling her mom. Another person might have done something else to settle down before getting back on the road.

When we're in a good frame of mind, our emotional system strives to keep us there. But nobody feels good all the time. We go through dozens of ups and downs every day in response to news, events, fatigue, and who knows what else. Most of these shifts are so small we barely notice them: our emotional system gets us back into balance that quickly. But bigger setbacks can drag people down. When something happens that throws us off balance, we need our emotional system to restore equilibrium

> *Dina worked at a busy florist shop. When a customer made a $46 purchase and handed her fifty dollars, Dina made change with four ones. One of the bills was folded over, so she mistakenly gave back only three dollars. The customer got angry and accused Dina of trying to cheat him. Dina knew it was a simple mistake and tried to explain, but the customer refused to believe her and stomped out.*
>
> *Dina felt terrible. Her sense of Oneness with her self-image as an honest person had been attacked. Immediately, her emotional system kicked in. She knew she had done nothing wrong, but reason alone did not stop the awful feeling. She asked the woman next in line to wait a moment and went out back. She closed her eyes, took a couple of deep breaths to relax and felt the emotional hurt like a heavy weight in her chest. Then she let the feeling go... simply let it drop. She put on a smile and stepped forward to wait on her next customer.*

On a busy day, we rarely stop to think about our emotional state. Only when something doesn't feel quite right are we likely to even notice our emotions at all.

I was traveling on a sightseeing boat in Argentina when an older man spoke to me. "I noticed you're an American," he said in a tentative voice. I was enjoying the scenery of the Andes and he wanted to talk about the differences between where we were and Indiana, where he lived. After he explained that this was only his second trip abroad, and that he would not meet up with his tour group until the next day, I understood. The man felt nervous about being far from home. Because I am American, I represented a link to the life he knew. He might not have chosen to talk to me under other circumstances, but on that boat, ten thousand miles from home, I was a beacon of familiarity in a sea of foreignness.

> Only when something doesn't feel quite right are we likely to even notice our emotions at all.

In a distant place, many familiar connections—people, places and activities—are absent. The man on the boat felt disconnected from what he was used to. Finding someone from "home" to talk to helped restore a piece of all that was missing: "At least *someone* here is like me."

A powerful, personal connection

Emotional Oneness is entirely experiential and personal. It occurs so frequently and in so many ways that we take it for granted and do not notice it most of the time. Oneness always feels fresh because feelings happen only in this moment right now. We can never store up good feelings and save them for later. Similarly, we cannot make someone else share our feeling of Oneness, no matter how hard we try.

All good, pleasurable feelings are aspects of Oneness, including love, happiness, joy, satisfaction and pleasure. When we imagine anything that is precious to us, any thing or person that we love, we evoke that central experience from which the rest of our emotional life flows,

> All good, pleasurable feelings are aspects of Oneness.

and toward which our emotional system is always trying to steer us. The quality of our life experience is directly related to the presence or absence of Oneness in its many forms.

Oneness exists in many realms. While each has its own unique characteristics, they fall into a few broad categories.

Oneness in personal relationships: Intimacy

At the level of personal relationships, Oneness feels like intimacy. You feel close to your beloved, your child or parent, your friend. That person arouses strong feelings of connection. The feeling may last a lifetime, or it may be as brief as a romantic fling. The feeling of intimacy tends to be intense and deep, and very personal.

Carlos and Clara started dating as teenagers and married in their early 20's. Their marriage was tested early on, but since their two sons were born, they have grown closer and closer. They enjoy each other's company immensely. At their recent "100th birthday party"—they both turned 50 the same month—Clara made Carlos sound like the ideal husband, because for her he is. Carlos summed up their relationship by saying, "I don't know exactly where I'm going. But I certainly know who I'm going there with."

This core potential for the experience of Oneness originated in the very first relationship you ever had. Before you became an individual person you were a part of your mother. In the biological sense, you and your mom were one physical being.

When you were born, helpless and dependent, you became separate, but your mother's feeling of connection with you did not go away. She held you, fed you and cared for you. Emotionally, she felt every bit as bonded with you after you separated physically from her as before.

As you grew up, your capacity for relationship took on new forms. You shared life with family and made close friends. In time you became part of other communities outside your family, as feelings of sympathetic togetherness with others filled your life. The feeling took on a variety of shapes: romance, affection for close friends, respect for mentors or colleagues. With each of them you had a satisfying bond of connection on an emotional level. The best of them felt the most intimate.

You discovered that every close relationship is unique. With one person you can talk about the most personal matters. With another you have a great time discussing sports, fashion or business. In a full life you can feel close to many people, each in his or her own distinct way.

Intimate relationships with family, friends and lovers are but the most obvious aspect of the powerful experience of Oneness. We also feel it when in happy alignment with a moment or a place or an idea.

Oneness with ideals: Transcendence

At the level of ideals and ideas, Oneness feels like transcendence. This feeling of closeness goes beyond the personal to a spiritual or religious connection. The purest moments of spiritual experience are based in an absolute connection with a higher Truth, or deeply aligned with a teacher or tradition, or in love with humanity. Holiness, with all that it implies, is at the heart of religious Oneness.

> "My friends tell me I have an intimacy problem. But they don't really know me."
> – GARRY SHANDLING, comedian

Times of deepest spiritual certainty can be life changing. If you have had such moments, you will never forget the perfect soul connection with God or whatever you call your spiritual ideal.

Freedom is an idea that generates transcendent feelings of Oneness. People identify so deeply with it that they will pay any price to preserve Freedom at home. A nation will send its young men and women to fight and die to help bring Freedom to other lands.

Why are people willing to risk their lives in the name of abstract ideals such as Freedom or a community's understanding of God? Because these ideals generate powerful feelings of connection and identity. We are willing to make extraordinary sacrifices to keep and sustain the bonds of Oneness they inspire.

Fred was on the 83rd floor of the World Trade Center on the morning of September 11, 2001. He claims he could see the face of the terrorist pilot just before the plane crashed into the building. Chaos and panic followed as burning jet fuel consumed an office just down the hall. Then, out of the smoke and madness, a firefighter appeared. The fireman calmly told everyone how to get down, which staircase would lead them to the ground floor and which would not. Fred and the others scrambled down dozens of flights of stairs in pitch darkness and emerged in the lobby just as the elevator shafts began to cave in. Four minutes after they made it outside, the entire building collapsed. The fireman who guided them was last seen headed upstairs to try to help save other stranded men and women.

> People have been willing to risk their lives in the name of abstract ideals, such as Freedom, or a community's particular understanding of God ... because these ideals generate powerful feelings of connection and identity.

18

The firefighter who gave his life that day acted out of a powerful commitment to his ideals. He had devoted himself to saving lives. In a crisis, allegiance to what he stood for transcended concerns for his personal safety. He honored his commitment that day and ultimately rescued dozens of people at the cost of his own life.

Love for your country or hometown, can also inspire transcendent feelings of Oneness. Love of country has much in common with the way we feel about our parents. Our homeland raised us and nurtured us. Unless it has betrayed us, we feel naturally connected to it. At the same time we also feel a bond with our countrymen and women who share that connection.

At the level of societies and nations, Oneness is expressed as peace. When large communities operate in harmony with one another, disagreements may arise but they do not lead to war.

> "Happiness is mostly a by-product of doing what makes us feel fulfilled."
> – DR. BENJAMIN SPOCK

Oneness with aspirations: Satisfaction

At the level of our aspirations, Oneness feels like satisfaction. When we accomplish what we set out to do we feel satisfied. Participating in activities we enjoy and sharing them with friends is satisfying too.

As a little boy, Dan loved cars and trucks. When he was twelve and his sister's boyfriend came to pick her up in a blue Corvette, he fell in love. "I can still see it in our driveway," he says. "It was sleek, bold, just waiting to roar to life." He has loved Corvettes ever since. As a teenager he joined the Corvette Club. The day he could finally afford to buy his first one was the happiest day of his life. Dan enjoys socializing with other Corvette owners and goes on driving trips with them. "It still gives me a thrill," he says.

Dan loves owning and driving a Corvette because it satisfies a personal aspiration. Possessions make us happy because they fulfill certain needs and desires. The things are material, but the needs and desires are not.

The fulfillment of personal aspirations is satisfying in all sorts of ways. A salesman who completes a big sale feels satisfied about earning money but also because he gets to see himself as a success at his job. An athlete or a musician feels satisfied after a strong performance because of a feeling of having achieved Oneness with the athlete or musician he or she has worked to become.

Achieving any goal you have truly wanted will be satisfying because it realizes a personal aspiration. If accomplishing a goal fails to satisfy, even for a short while, chances are the goal was not what you really wanted in the first place.

Oneness with self: Confidence and contentment

At the level of self, Oneness feels like confidence and contentment. This could be the most important dimension of all, the feeling of wholeness within yourself. These are the adult version of your newborn days when you were fed, held and content in the embrace of your mother or father.

When in harmony within ourselves and feeling content, our minds are clear of confusion and doubt. We are open and can direct our attention outward to

> "How I relate to my inner self influences my relationships with all others. My satisfaction with myself and my satisfaction with other people are directly proportional."
> – SUE ATCHLEY EBAUGH, author

people and events around us. Only when we are unhappy or struggling do we focus inward and think about how we are doing and how we feel.

Paul is never quite satisfied with himself. He is bright, well-spoken, and attractive, but inside he feels inadequate. Whatever he accomplishes, he always thinks about what he might have done better. His dissatisfaction is a nagging voice that torments him, and has done so for as long as he can remember.

Paul would like to get married and settle down. Many women find him charming but he lacks the confidence to approach the ones he finds most attractive, and so he goes out with less interesting women until he gets bored. He sees himself as his own worst enemy.

Paul's feelings of inadequacy leave him out of touch with the man he would like to be or thinks he should be. He can imagine someone else in exactly the same situation being happy, but he is not.

Virtually all of us go through periods of being out of sync with ourselves, as Paul is, especially during the difficult transitional years of growing up. We make choices that seem reasonable, but then change our minds. Or circumstances force us to live a life that is not of our own choosing. Or we simply don't know what we want.

Finding balance within yourself is a precious skill, especially in challenging times. The last chapter of this book talks about self love

OTHER USES OF THE TERM "ONENESS"

The term "Oneness" has been used in many contexts, especially to suggest harmony with higher spiritual realms. Religious leaders talk about Oneness in reference to the indivisibility of God. It has been used to argue against prejudice, especially racism. A spiritual movement based in India has created the "Oneness movement" and a "Oneness University" to teach spiritual growth and fulfillment.

"Oneness" in this text is intended strictly in an emotional sense. It's a powerful emotional feeling of connection, bonding or harmony and not related to any religious or social tradition. Oneness refers exclusively to the set of positive, connected feelings at the center of the emotional system as described in this chapter.

and offers guidance on how to find inner harmony and the road to Oneness with self.

Stop, look, feel

If you have been reading this far without stopping to feel for yourself what Oneness feels like, you are missing the point. None of this, and none of what follows, can be understood as ideas only. You have to pause long enough to look into your own emotions.

Think about one person for whom you have strong, powerful feelings of affection. Picture that person in your mind right now. Let your affection for that person arise naturally, and feel what happens in your heart. Notice the feelings of connection, like emotional fingers that reach out and link you with the object of your affection. This is Oneness.

Or imagine yourself doing a favorite activity or enjoying your favorite food. Imagine yourself skiing or eating chocolate, wearing your most comfortable jeans or sitting in your favorite chair. Picture yourself watching a spectacular summer sunset or your favorite team in your favorite sport.

> Oneness at its best feels like love.

Oneness is a great feeling: whole, complete, perhaps in love, but in any event strongly connected to something or someone you care about. That feeling is the starting point for understanding all emotion and the key to passing through moments of upset back to feelings of contentment and satisfaction.

The root of all emotion

Oneness is the core emotional experience from which everything else arises. *All our feelings, the full range of our emotional life, reflect being in some harmonious Oneness bond or are a response to its absence.* Emotions are infinitely complex, subtle and fleeting, but the *source* of feeling, the presence or absence of Oneness, is simple.

Oneness at its best feels like love. In the intricate, subtle, ever-changing human emotional system, Oneness is both where you start from and where you want to end up.

Try this: Try to identify something you have in common with a person you might feel uncomfortable around. It can be anything at all. Does awareness of sharing some piece of the human experience, a bit of Oneness, inspire a sense of connection? Does it generate a more positive feeling ?

Summary

- All good feelings reflect an emotional connection or state of harmony with people, ideals, or other component of life.
- This state of emotional connection and harmony is called Oneness.
- All human emotion arises from some aspect of Oneness feeling, or reflects its loss or absence.

CHAPTER 3

Sorrowing: The Emotional System Seeks *Resolution*

When we experience a loss, when we are sad or hurt or disappointed, when we feel let down, abandoned or discouraged and the feeling won't go away, there is a process that can soften, even heal emotional pain. It's called *sorrowing*.

> *Bart, a commercial photographer, bid on an assignment to shoot a corporate annual report for a large multinational. The job would entail overseas travel, and he was excited about doing it. He researched the company carefully and put in the lowest bid he could.*
>
> *The designer on the project loved the proposal and Bart's sample pictures. Bart was sure he would get the job. When he found out*

that it had been given to someone else, he was crestfallen. He wondered what had gone wrong.

Should he have shown a different portfolio? Did he call the designer too frequently, or not often enough? He imagined that the photographer who got the job might be paying a kickback, or perhaps she and the designer were old buddies. Maybe Bart's level of work was just not very good. Maybe he was destined to be a failure.

None of this thinking helped Bart feel better or get back to work finding new clients. But he couldn't stop thinking about it. Eventually, he plopped down in a chair, sighed, and acknowledged how disappointed he felt. He let himself drift deep into feelings of sorrow, and forced himself to stay in that unhappy place. It felt miserable, but he had to get to the bottom of his feeling of loss and rejection.

When he finally emerged he was tired, but something had shifted. Recovery had begun. Bart quit work early and took the evening off. When thoughts of the annual report drifted through his mind, he just let them be there and noticed how he felt. The next morning he was still unhappy about losing the annual report, but he was no longer immobilized. He was able to pick up the phone and start looking for more work.

> Sorrowing can soften, even heal emotional pain.

Bart knew that feelings are impermanent. Today's discouragement is temporary and will yield to a different set of emotions tomorrow.

The time is now

The emotional system operates in the short term: feelings happen only right now. Just as we breathe to get oxygen into our blood now, our emotional system acts to make us feel better in the current moment. It does not take into account how we might feel an hour from now, next week, or in ten years.

Feelings are created and recreated moment by moment. When we feel generally happy or sad for a while, what is really happening is that we feel that way now, and again now, and again now. In this respect feelings are like muscle fibers that do not stay rigidly flexed but fire again and again in rapid sequence to keep the muscle tight, until eventually fatigue sets in. Our emotional state renews itself constantly in response to changes in ourselves and our environment. That is why it is impossible to make a pleasant feeling last any longer than its time.

This narrow focus on the current moment stabilizes us but can come at a cost. It can make us ignore feelings that merit deeper consideration in favor of a temporarily more comfortable state.

At 22, Max had finally decided to attend college full time. With limited savings and his parents unable to help, he applied for a scholarship with high expectations. His heart sank when his scholarship request was rejected.

Thinking about filling out loan applications and taking on a lot of debt made Max's head spin. He opened a beer and watched sports on TV all night to avoid thinking about his problem. The next morning, he considered calling his buddies to find some fun activity, but thought better of it. He went to the library and devoted that day and the next to applying for financial aid, and eventually got the assistance he needed.

At first, Max dealt with feeling disappointed by distracting himself. In the short term, his emotional system protected him from suffering by making him feel better instead of terrible about not getting the scholarship. Max knew he would eventually have to do something he did not care to do—research options and fill out paperwork—but he was unable to face it right away.

What is the right time to address hurt feelings and resolve uncomfortable emotions? Right now is best. If that is too difficult, the sooner the better. Max could afford to wait a day to go back to work finding a college loan. He knew he could not wait too long.

Getting back to oneness: Sorrowing

A dynamic system that falls out of balance naturally tries to restore its equilibrium. When the emotional system gets out of balance, when we feel emotionally out of sorts, we want to resolve the disharmony.

The most direct and effective way to resolve painful or unpleasant feelings is the process called sorrowing. Sorrowing is the explicit processing of unpleasant feelings by addressing them head on and feeling them all the way through. It is generally uncomfortable and can be quite painful. It might take only a few moments or last much longer. You may not be able to do it all at once and may have to revisit it over time. It is hard to know in advance how long it will last or when it will be finished. You will know internally, on a purely emotional level, when it is over.

> Sorrowing is the explicit processing of unpleasant feelings by addressing them head on and feeling them all the way through.

At first glance, this sounds awful. Why would anyone want to feel hurtful feelings on purpose? The answer is simple: addressing painful feelings this way is the fastest, most permanent way to put them behind us.

Emotions we cannot accept or "be with" have power over us. When we open ourselves to them and work through them, they lose that power. Through sorrowing we make peace with emotional pain and free ourselves to move forward.

Sorrowing is paradoxical: it restores us to enjoyable feelings by facing up to difficult feelings. By leaning into what feels bad, we prepare ourselves to feel good. It is our most valuable tool in the journey back to feelings of Oneness.

If you remember only one principle from this entire book, this is the one to remember. Sorrowing heals emotional pain. Learn the power of appropriate sorrowing to heal emotional wounds.

Sorrowing works equally as well on momentary events that hurt our feelings as it does for long-held emotions of loss or failure that somehow won't go away. The scale is different but the process is the same.

The way little children process loss and hurt provides a helpful example:

> *My daughter was playing at the beach with other children. She was scooping out sand in her pail, building a big sand castle, until one of the boys playing nearby drove his plastic truck right through her creation and demolished it.*
>
> *My daughter shrieked and wailed. I picked her up to comfort her as she sobbed. She clung to me for barely a minute. Then she saw another child she wanted to play with. She asked to be put down, and off she went. The loss of her sand castle, and her sorrowing over it, were finished and forgotten.*

Sorrowing is a uniquely personal process. Once you've done it successfully a few times, you'll have a better idea of how it works for you.

> **Sorrowing is a uniquely personal process.**

Emotional processing has to be appropriate to the scale of the injury. Some people go to the gym or throw themselves into work, gardening or household tasks. A friend's father who lived in Washington, D.C. would settle his upset feelings by driving the Beltway, a ring road around the city. When he was especially upset, he would drive two complete circuits.

> *Hideki lost his only son in the World Trade Center attacks in 2001. His son was at work for a financial firm on the top floor of one of the towers when the airplanes struck. He never had a chance.*
>
> *Hideki is a runner. He runs a few miles every day and has for many years. Running has always been therapeutic for him, relaxing his mind and giving him time to think without interruptions. After his son's death, running became Hideki's vehicle for processing his grief. For many months I used to see him out running in the morning, tears streaming down his face.*

> Intentional sorrowing—the deliberate processing of painful emotion—is the key to coming to terms with suffering.

Sorrowing heals suffering. That is why it is the linchpin of the entire emotional system. Intentional sorrowing—the deliberate processing of painful emotion—is the key to coming to terms with suffering.

A personal story in ordinary sorrowing

I used to coach basketball. For two years I coached the freshman girls team at a nearby high school. My job was to help 14-year old girls develop their basketball skills and to mature as individuals and team players. It paid little but was enjoyable and very gratifying.

When the head varsity coach called one summer morning to tell me that he had hired a young woman to replace me, I felt very sad. I understood that it made more sense to have as coach a woman in her 20's who had recently played college basketball than a man in his 50's who had not. I knew I was not being fired for doing a bad job or for being a jerk. Still, I felt the sharp feeling of loss.

The experience was emotionally painful. I thought about what a terrific team we had had the previous year, and how grateful I was for that. I reminisced about wild bus rides on cold winter afternoons to away games and practices that ended in laughter. I knew I would miss coaching, and mostly, I would miss the girls.

I spent that whole day letting myself feel sad whenever sadness arose. I did not indulge the emotion or feel sorry for myself. I allowed the feeling to wash through me just as it was whenever it occurred, which was often that day.

I noticed a tendency to want to blame someone for my loss, though there was nobody to blame. The coach had made a decision he considered in the interest of the program. It was not about me. I did not try to convince myself that it was really all for the best in some greater sense. At times my thinking scurried to find a silver lining to this loss, as if by finding something good my hurt feelings would be diminished. These are all normal kinds of thoughts people have after a loss.

Whenever basketball coaching floated up in my imagination that day, I simply let the emotion sit there. I sighed a lot. My family treated me with extra compassion, which I appreciated. Occasionally they tried to cheer me up by reminding me that I had done a good job and that the change wasn't because of my fault or failure. While I was grateful for the kindness behind their words, awkward attempts to make me feel better made me uncomfortable since I knew my hurt feelings were perfectly legitimate.

I was more irritable that day than usual. I simply did not feel like talking to people. When I went to bed that night, I thought again about losing the coaching job, and felt sad about it.

The next morning, I was a bit less sad. The loss weighed less heavily on my mind. I sent a quick note to the varsity coach thanking him for the opportunity of the previous years and for his honesty in telling me about the change. What else could I do? I had compassion for his extreme discomfort in having to call me with bad news.

> "Success is going from failure to failure without a loss of enthusiasm."
> – WINSTON CHURCHILL

I sorrowed over the loss because that's all there was to do with it. Each day I thought about it less frequently than the day before. After about four days, I felt I had made my peace with it. The sting of the loss was gone and my self-esteem was not beaten down by the rejection. I would have taken the job back in a minute, but it had stopped being an emotional burden.

By sorrowing over this loss in a clear, direct way, I processed the feelings and (mostly) completed them. How much longer might I have felt badly about what happened had I responded differently?

I could have protested. I could have blamed myself for not having been a good enough coach, or blamed others for not noticing what a good job I had done. I could have scrambled to find another team, with the hope of getting revenge by beating my previous team. I could have tried to distract myself with a flurry of activity or a few drinks just to dodge the uncomfortable emotions. I might have concluded that I was really a much worse coach and a much bigger failure than I had realized. Or I could have stuffed down the hurt so I would not have to feel it at all.

That is not how sorrowing works. None of those activities would have returned me to Oneness with a positive self-image of myself as a competent and good person as quickly or effectively.

Stuck feelings and old wounds

For most of us, the emotional system does its job reasonably well most of the time without our even noticing it. Like white blood cells fighting off infection, it gets us past feelings of hurt, rejection and disappointment with only minor discomfort. Through strategic sorrowing over whatever unpleasant emotions remain, we free ourselves to restore emotional balance and move on.

Occasionally, however, the system stumbles and emotions get stuck. Feelings of hurt and loss— the product of who-knows-what events and the resulting thoughts, decisions and conclusions— embed themselves deep in our consciousness where they influence our behavior, even alter our personality.

COGNITIVE DISSONANCE THEORY

Cognitive Dissonance is a long-accepted psychological theory that explains what people tend to do when two simultaneously held thoughts, beliefs, attitudes or behaviors contradict each other. Created by Leon Festinger in 1957, the theory of cognitive dissonance states that a person will act to reduce dissonance—the tension between the two incompatible sides—in an effort to avoid feelings of distress. Festinger considered the need to reduce dissonance as basic as any other need such as hunger.

Aesop's fable about the fox and the grapes is a perfect example. The fox hungers for grapes that are beyond his reach. After struggling unsuccessfully to get the grapes, the fox eventually decides that the grapes were probably sour anyway. Wanting the grapes and being unable to get them caused the dissonance or discrepancy. The fox resolved it by changing his opinion of the grapes to make them less desirable rather than endure the feeling of failure because he couldn't reach them.

Cognitive dissonance theory explains why I felt like blaming the head coach for replacing me. Good coaches don't get fired, right? Therefore, since I was fired, I could only reduce the dissonance by deciding either that I was a bad coach and deserved to be fired, or that the person who fired me was an idiot. Not wanting to think of myself as a failure, it would be easy to criticize the other guy.

We can apply cognitive dissonance theory to many ordinary situations. Imagine liking person A and disliking person B, then finding out they are best friends. What do you do? Do you decrease your liking of A or reconsider by concluding that maybe B isn't so bad? If you go on a date with someone you find attractive who won't see you a second time, do you think less of yourself or less highly of the person who snubbed you?

Cognitive dissonance theory explains why we have certain uncomfortable feelings sometimes. It does not tell us how to get back to feeling better. Most of the time, appropriate sorrowing restores Oneness and heals feelings of loss and discomfort more effectively than shifting our point of view simply to reduce tension.

Michael remembers the day when he asked a child's innocent question at the Thanksgiving table and everyone laughed. He could not have been more than eight years old. He doesn't remember the question, but he remembers how it hurt his feelings to be laughed at. He also recalls then and there making a decision not to ask questions he didn't already know the answer to.

Michael became a quiet child. To this day, he has little to say. While coworkers at his accounting firm have been more aggressive and have advanced, Michael's career has languished. It is still hard for him to ask for guidance or seek help from others in addressing problems.

For stuck, painful feelings, time stands still. Michael had completely forgotten the childhood incident that helped shape his personality. Not until he was so unhappy that he was motivated to look deeper, working with a psychotherapist, did he even discover it.

Old emotional wounds often stem from childhood events. Even incidents that seem trivial to others can make a deep mark on a child's psyche. The social challenges of the teenage years and into adulthood also can leave deep scars.

> We all carry a store of deep, buried emotion.

We all carry a store of deep, buried emotion. We can't help it. We have the power to choose what, if anything, to do about them.

Anna shared a young girl's fantasy of getting married, having a family, and living happily in a big house, but her life didn't turn out that way. Her first husband had a drinking problem and her next husband-to-be ended the engagement just weeks before the wedding date.

Anna gathered her courage and turned her attention to her work. She became a successful novelist and enjoyed a good life until she went home, one day, looked in the mirror, and saw the face of a wounded woman. As she looked at herself, all the rejection and disappointment of her broken childhood dreams rose up to greet her.

Anna decided she had to come to terms with years of being brave and stuffing down emotions. She made characters in her books work through some of the same difficulties she had struggled with. Writing was the path that helped Anna process and heal old wounds. When she looked back at her earliest writing, she was surprised to find characters who struggled with the same issues.

Who hasn't been wounded by rejection and failure? Who doesn't have stories to tell? One of the most effective ways to work through old wounds is by telling our stories, actually recounting what happened, either verbally or in writing. The story does not need to be published or broadcast to a wide audience. It helps to have one listener who really listens.

Mandy's parents were divorced before she was a year old. She was raised by her father, who jealously protected her from spending time with her mom. It was awkward. Many times when other kids would be with their moms, Mandy felt left out. After she finished high school, Mandy sought out and got to know her mom. As they talked, she found they both had many stories to tell.

Mandy shared what it was like growing up without a mother's tenderness or a female role model. She explained how hard it had been to learn from her father what she needed to know about boys. Mandy talked out the story of her life as her mother listened eagerly. Then her mom shared what it was like knowing she had a daughter whose growing-up years she would never see.

Telling their stories was healing to them both. It allowed them to release some of the pain of the past and turn their attention to creating a new relationship in the present.

We can't magically make stuck emotions disappear. But we can avoid accumulating more. We can stop burying painful emotions going forward by processing feelings of hurt and loss in the moment so that they do not become stuck. Over time we can also begin to root out existing deep wounded feelings and loosen ourselves from their grip.

Sorrowing, in the appropriate form, processes old wounds as well as current disappointments. It can help clear up painful buried feelings, even if we can't identify them one by one. When we work through old feelings of hurt and loss, we make peace with even a painful and difficult early history.

> "You're never too old to have a happy childhood."
> – TOM ROBBINS, novelist

Sorrowing through the arts

Have you ever had a good cry at the movies? Been touched by a character in a novel or moved by a symphony? The arts stir us because they evoke feelings that may not be accessible otherwise. If you cry at a film because the heroine dies at the end, you are not crying for an actress's screen death. The tears mean that what happened onscreen evoked feelings from somewhere inside you. You gave the film permission to touch you. You used that opportunity to cry out some of your own wounded feelings buried deep inside.

People have the capacity for empathy, the ability to imagine other people's feelings. For someone's situation to affect us enough to make us cry, it must touch an emotion from our own personal history. The next time you cry at a movie or are touched by a piece of music, consider that this art form may be evoking some of your own buried feelings.

Processing hidden feelings by responding emotionally to artistic expressions of other people's experiences actually works. We feel lighter and cleaner after a good cry. A fan of singer/songwriter Joni Mitchell's music once said to her, "Before there was Prozac, there were your songs."

The sorrow point

Sometimes you can find the exact center of a feeling of loss, anger or fear. When you re-experience the precise moment when the feeling occurred, you've found the sorrow point.

The sorrow point is the place of direct access to the source of an unpleasant emotion. By processing the emotion at the sorrow point you have the best chance to complete a painful or upsetting feeling before it gets stuck.

> *Ian blundered in a presentation at work and said something inappropriate about a colleague. He was trying to be funny, but his words landed badly. He felt terrible about it. His apology afterward was awkward.*
>
> *Ian was unhappy with himself the rest of the day. He could not shake a nagging voice of self-criticism. Only once he got home could he fully re-imagine his dumb remark and the emotions it generated. He concentrated all his attention on that moment, the sorrow point, and re-experienced the moment when he recognized his mistake. Rather than judge himself, he stayed with the emotion for as long as it took. By focusing on that emotional moment, he released his guilt, and the nagging voice in his head stopped. He resolved to try to mend what damage he had caused and to make an effort to be wiser about how he spoke at work from then on.*

Ian knew he was not a bad person; he had just made a mistake. By going to the sorrow point quickly and processing the feeling thoroughly, he prevented negative judgments and conclusions about himself from lingering in his consciousness.

The sorrow point is most likely to be available in clear-cut situations like Ian's when one specific moment causes the upsetting emotion. Complex situations with many sources or multifaceted concerns that have lasted a long time tend not to have a single sorrow point.

Clearing feelings

Mark goes for a walk in the woods near his home every morning. Sometimes he thinks about the issues of the day or his business. Most of the time he takes advantage of the stillness and lets his thoughts and feelings drift.

Mark may describe a day's walk as sad or melancholy, but be unable to explain why. His emotional system is doing what it should, clearing up points of emotional upset to make his life better. Some walks he enjoys more than others. Over time he has said that the morning walks have played an important role in making him more content.

The process of clearing feelings intentionally requires setting aside quiet time from a busy schedule. Those who are constantly driven to do and achieve may have no precedent for exploring the internal landscape of reflection and sorrowing. Finding a balance between outer achievement and inner peace is central to generating a truly satisfying and fulfilling life.

Sorrowing is, by its very nature, an internal process. Emotional healing only happens in the deep recesses of our own heart and soul. If we were skilled at sorrowing, we would always devote just the right amount of ourselves to healing each significant painful loss, and we would quickly get on with life. As a practical matter, getting it right all the time is just about impossible. It is hard to recognize deep feelings that can come from any direction, and it is hard to know exactly what to do with them.

> "Successful people... make it a habit to do the things unsuccessful people don't like to do."
> – CYNTHIA FARSADI, businesswoman

The courage to begin

It takes courage and commitment to face up to difficult, painful emotions. While it is easy to find excuses, taking the hard steps and doing the inner work leads to a better future.

Try this: The next time you notice feeling emotionally bruised—rejected or disappointed—look inside for the sorrow point. Recall the exact moment when a piece of bad news or someone's words triggered the feeling of hurt. Focus on your *feeling* of that moment. You don't have to do anything to change it. See if this process doesn't help release the charge of that emotion and allow you to move beyond it.

43

Summary

- Sorrowing is the active process of working through feelings of loss.
- Sorrowing is the most effective way to complete emotional suffering.
- In sorrowing we go to the emotional core of a feeling, which releases its charge and allows us to move beyond it.
- We all have a weight of buried hurt feelings that we can begin to lift by appropriate sorrowing.

CHAPTER 4

The Art of the Truth

It can be surprisingly difficult to answer the simple question "How do I feel right now?" We find many attractive reasons to mislead or confuse ourselves. A necessary element of emotional health, however, is the ability to see beyond how we'd like to feel or think we "should" feel, and acknowledge truly how we really do feel at any given moment.

There are many reasons why we often find this challenging. They include:

- We are not in the habit of acknowledging feelings. Our parents didn't do that, we weren't raised that way, we've never done it.
- We don't pay attention and therefore have no way of knowing how we feel.
- We dislike unpleasant emotions and would rather not acknowledge them.

- We are afraid that if we recognize that we feel bad, it will make us feel worse.
- We think it's not right to wallow in our emotions.
- We worry that recognizing bad feelings will slow us down.
- We worry that if we admit to feeling terrific we might undermine or wreck it.
- We are invested in consistency. Strong emotion risks upsetting our stability.
- We don't trust ourselves to be able to deal with uncomfortable feelings.
- We are seduced by media messages that we are supposed to be happy all the time.

> A necessary element of emotional health is the ability to see beyond how we'd like to feel or think we "should" feel, and acknowledge truly how we really *do* feel.

Virtually all of these decisions happen below our conscious awareness. Most of the time we are simply not aware that we are being less than fully truthful with ourselves. To improve our long term emotional well-being, we have to learn to accurately identify the current state of our feelings.

How do we begin? By noticing what is actually going on in the moment, whether or not we like or want it. One of the best and easiest ways to do this is through mindfulness.

Mindfulness

Techniques of mindfulness have been used for centuries to align thinking and feeling with current reality. Historically associated with Eastern religious traditions, mindfulness has made its way into Western thought as a valuable tool to settle the mind and relax the body. It is something anyone can do.

Mindfulness is the act of consciously focusing attention on what is actually happening right now, internally and externally. You notice and pay attention to exactly what you perceive in this moment and describe that without interpretation or judgment. It includes awareness through physical senses (vision, hearing, taste, smell and touch) in addition to thinking and includes rapid shifts in the focus of your attention. Here is an example:

> "Let us not look back in anger, nor forward in fear, but around us in awareness."
> – JAMES THURBER, humorist and author

I am looking out through the window at four tall trees. The leaves are dark green, and sunlight plays across the trunk of one of the trees but not the other three. A squirrel runs between the two closest trees and off to the left. I feel my seat in the chair and my fingers typing this. The computer keyboard clicks with each letter. My left shoulder feels tense and I relax the muscle allowing the shoulder to drop. One foot is resting flat on the

*floor and the other is on its side. There is a rumbling sound of
a truck outside. I smell a whiff of diesel fumes through the open
window. My shoulder feels tense again.*

There is nothing tricky about mindfulness: it's quite ordinary. Since the mind moves quickly, a mindfulness exercise can cover many individual observations in a very short time. Any kind of observation is okay, including observations about observations (for example, noticing that I am thinking about whether I am spelling the words in this sentence correctly).Whenever your mind drifts to ordinary, sequential kinds of thinking, which it surely will do, you can gently bring it back to whatever sensations and awareness you notice in the moment.

Mindfulness is essentially a relaxation technique. As our thinking focuses on bits of what is going on around and within us, we don't think about other matters. Worries and fears recede, at least for the moment. We do not have to decide what to do about whatever we see, hear and feel. If we turn our attention to taking long, deep breaths and

> Mindfulness is essentially a relaxation technique.

just observe our breath going in and out, both mind and body relax. Even our emotional state becomes more tranquil as our attention is consumed by noticing the small details of breath, thinking and physical senses.

Mindfulness is useful in this context because it is an exercise in truth-telling. Through the practice of describing small things accurately and in detail, we learn the habit of acknowledging the simple truth without embellishment. The ability to report exactly what is going on without judgment helps us to recognize our current emotions. Professor Charles Tart of the University of California at Davis says: "Becoming mindful, observing and remembering yourself, being increasingly sensitive to the exact nature of your reactions to the world, allows...greater sensitivity to your genuine, essential feelings."

> "Becoming mindful, observing and remembering yourself, being increasingly sensitive to the exact nature of your reactions to the world, allows... greater sensitivity to your genuine, essential feelings."
> – PROFESSOR CHARLES TART

Mindfulness can become a form of meditation that benefits from daily practice. Like other forms of meditation, it brings calm and relaxation to offset the stress of a busy life. Mindfulness has the added advantage of encouraging truth-telling in situations where it may be difficult to sort out complicated or contradictory feelings. It's a great tool to help answer the question, "How do I feel?" in moments of conflict or confusion.

You can practice mindfulness any time. Walking down the street, mindfulness lets you see physical details and hear sounds you might never have noticed, even if you have walked that street many times. In that respect, mindfulness can be both refreshing and entertaining.

It is especially valuable for people with busy minds.

Authenticity inside and out

The practice of mindfulness brings us in closer touch with our current inner emotional state. It grounds us in what is true at this moment and aligns our thoughts and feelings. Such alignment makes us more authentic, both internally and in relation to others.

Authenticity means being emotionally integrated down to the core: our thoughts, words and deeds truly reflect our inner being. We feel whole and balanced when we are being authentic. We also tend to be most comfortable around others whom we perceive as being authentic.

> Authenticity means being emotionally integrated down to the core.

When someone you're talking to is authentic, you can sense it. There is an inherent integrity in how they present themselves. Their words are credible because you perceive that what they are saying and doing truthfully reflects their character and inner emotional state. Contrast that to when a speaker's words sound false or insincere, when words appear to belie emotions. It can be jarring.

Joanna was a lovely woman who smiled constantly. She was enthusiastic about her job and quick to describe her exercise program. Her laugh was harsh. I felt uncomfortable around her from the moment I met her.

Joanna could be fun at parties, but I was exhausted after spending time with her. Only after she became seriously ill, I learned that her only daughter had been killed in a car crash the week after she got her driver's license. As often happens after the death of a child, Joanna's marriage fell apart shortly thereafter.

In the aftermath of her tragedy, Joanna was determined to stay upbeat. She read books and attended seminars on how to maintain a positive attitude after personal tragedy. She used willpower to keep an upbeat attitude most of the time, but her life was a lie. Inside she was heartbroken. She exercised too much to stave off sad feelings and drank to numb the pain.

Joanna could not be authentic because the voice of pain inside her was trapped by her well-meaning determination to stay positive. Nobody blames her for trying so hard. Her friends make a special effort to treat her with compassion.

I knew a woman who seemed to be in love with love but the feeling was fragile. She hugged a lot of people and told them that she loved them. Underneath she was lonely. Trying to solve feelings of emptiness did not work because Oneness is impossible to fake. We know this intuitively. Yet inauthenticity is all around us. In part, this happens because it is difficult to balance social norms—how we think we're supposed to interact with others—with subtle feelings that may be hard to recognize or understand.

Marilyn was an acting student in London in the 1970s. Fans of theater would come around her school to attend plays and hobnob with the actors. Because she was attractive and skilled, Marilyn drew her share of attention. Well-to-do strangers would say, "Oh you must come over to lunch one day." But they never named a date and never told her where they lived. Marilyn soon realized that these people felt a social obligation to make such offers, but they were not authentic. Her wealthy admirers never had any intention of following through.

Very young children tend to be authentic before they learn how they are "supposed" to behave. Older adults often become more consistently authentic once they have had enough life experience to know who they are. Self-knowledge is more difficult for those in their teens and twenties who have not had the time and experience to sort out their feelings and identities.

> "The funny thing about getting older is you really do get wiser."
> – JANE FONDA, actress, upon reaching middle age.

The better you know yourself, the easier it becomes to be authentic, and the more likely you are to notice when you are out of touch with your inner being. Speaking authentically feels different than saying what you hope is true or think might be true. People around you will hear the difference and so will you.

Making sense of feelings

There is always a reason why we feel the way we do. Professor Martha C. Nussbaum, in *Upheavals of Thought: the Intelligence of Emotions*, says that every emotion we feel has a story behind it. She writes: "The understanding of any emotion is incomplete unless its narrative history is grasped and studied for the light it sheds on the current response."

In trying to make sense of difficult emotions—understanding why we feel the way we do—we can sometimes tell that story accurately, sometimes not. When we discover the truth, it sets us free to fully understand what happened, to learn from the experience, and eventually to move on.

Nussbaum goes on to suggest that music is especially helpful in working through confusing emotions. Rather than making sense of a feeling via its story, the abstract quality of music touches emotions directly by bypassing linear patterns of verbal thinking. Who hasn't used music to settle jangled nerves?

Optimism

An optimistic attitude makes us stronger emotionally. Regardless of what is going on in our daily lives, maintaining a cheerful outlook lifts our spirits. Optimistic people bounce back from adversity more quickly, since they understand that setbacks are temporary and there is always something good to look forward to.

> "The road that is built in hope is more pleasant to the traveler than the road built in despair, even though they both lead to the same destination."
> – MARION ZIMMER BRADLEY, author

A pessimistic outlook makes ordinary tasks tougher. The expectation of unhappy consequences makes it harder to muster the enthusiasm to take chances and try new things. I've also learned to be wary of those who look you in the eye and say, "I'm a realist," then go on to recount how bad a situation is. They are some of the most committed pessimists of all.

We have a choice about how we understand what happens. Once we acknowledge the truth about current reality, we get to decide what it means and imagine where it will lead. A positive attitude helps us to keep moving forward and to interpret ambiguous results in a more satisfying way.

How we interpret what *has* happened in our world often influences what *will* happen next, and how such events are likely to affect us.

Sabrina teaches in an elementary school. She has a great variety of children in her class, those who behave well and those who cannot help but be disruptive. Sabrina's attitude is to see the best in every student. She imagines her students at their best and talks to them in terms of that image most of the time. The children usually respond. They behave better in her class than elsewhere. She still sometimes has to address behavior problems, but she never labels anyone as a bad kid or a troublemaker. For children who have struggled with behavior, Sabrina's positive attitude gives them a chance to grow out of their old identities and into becoming the terrific kids she holds them to be.

Sabrina's optimistic attitude did not just happen by accident. She chose to see her students that way because she understood that their emotional habits and their conclusions about themselves need not limit their potential.

Sabrina is not blind to the challenges some of her students bring, but she chooses not to give them more attention than is absolutely necessary. Her approach is consistent with the "Behaviorist" school of psychology, associated with B.F. Skinner and others. The Behaviorists claimed that "whatever you give attention to, you get more of." Paying attention to a pattern of behavior, favorable or otherwise, reinforces that behavior. Sabrina prefers to reinforce the good behavior. Her approach works with adults, too.

Obstacles to truthfulness

Most people consider themselves honest most of the time, but there are obstacles to being entirely truthful within ourselves. Some common obstacles to being as truthful as we might be include ignorance, habits, judgments, conclusions and beliefs.

Ignorance. Ignorance is simply not knowing. There is much we don't know yet, even about our own feelings. Often, admitting that we are uncertain is the first step to answering the question, "How do I feel?"

When we want to learn about the outside world, we look, listen, ask questions and pursue answers. But learning about our inner world happens in a completely different way. Internally, patience and asking the same questions again and again are more likely to lead to answers. Repeating the same simple inner questions helps us sort through layers of feelings and ideas to get to a deeper truth. The first step is to recognize that we simply don't know.

Habits. Habits regulate a substantial majority of what we do every day. They are enormously powerful. Because of our habits, we don't have to figure out how to do ordinary tasks all over again. Most habits make life easier and free our minds to focus on whatever is new, different and challenging.

> The differences in personality from one person to the next are in large part the sum total of our emotional habits.

We have emotional habits too, ways we typically respond to certain kinds of situations. Some people cry easily, others get angry at the slightest provocation. Some respond to emergencies with cool presence of mind while others panic. Some people feel guilty all the time and use guilt to motivate themselves. Others hardly ever feel guilty.

Emotional habits are at the core of each person's image of self. Antonio Damasio says, "Humans have developed a self-image mainly to establish a homeostatic organism." That means that our image of ourselves is critical to remaining stable in an ever-changing world. The differences in personality from one person to the next are in large part the sum total of our emotional habits.

Many emotional bad habits grew up at some point to make us feel better in the short term. Our emotional system, doing its job, favored immediate resolution of uncomfortable feelings, even though doing so may have led to unwelcome patterns later on.

When Alicia drives, she comments frequently about other drivers. "What's your hurry?" she shouts at a driver who pulls out in front of her. "How about today?" she says to someone who does not start up fast enough after the light turns green. Riding with Alicia is a running commentary on other drivers' mistakes and potentially dangerous maneuvers.

When asked about the origins of this habit, Alicia had to stop and think. Eventually it dawned on her: "That's what my father always did." She had learned about driving while riding with her parents and had simply adopted her dad's habit of talking about other drivers. He might have learned it from his father.

Alicia bore no grudge against other drivers. She was merely in the habit of responding this way. Even once she under-

stood where the habit came from, she continued her running monologue whenever she had a passenger in the car available to listen.

Emotional habits get worn into our psyche like grooves in a dirt road. Every time we repeat a habitual action or emotional response, we reinforce the habit as the groove becomes a little deeper. It takes deliberate action to do things differently.

> We never really get rid of old habits, but we can replace them with new ones by conscious decision and effort.

We never completely get rid of old habits. However, we can replace them with new ones. It takes conscious repetition to replace an old groove that has become a deep rut with a new and more effective behavior. In time, the new groove deepens and following it becomes more automatic, replacing the old, undesirable one.

Tommy still attends Alcoholics Anonymous meetings a couple of times a week, though he has not had a drink in over 20 years. He understands the power alcohol has had over him. He knows that the root of his old drinking habit still resides somewhere inside him. Tommy has led a remarkable life since he stopped drinking. He is one of the most courageous people I know.

The commitment to replace destructive habits with beneficial ones is powerful, and worthy of anyone who wants a better life. To change emotional habits, you first have to recognize you have a choice: the old, harmful habit isn't who you really are, it's just something you've been doing until now.

It helps to plan ahead so we are prepared when the trigger to the old habit appears. Then experiment with the new behavior even while the old habit tries to reassert itself. Though you may feel pulled in two directions at once, remember that you are "grooving" a new emotional habit.

> *George was in the habit of procrastinating until the last minute, then motivating himself to action by pumping himself up with pep talks and caffeine. He said he worked best under pressure. He got a lot accomplished this way, but at a cost. He usually finished tasks exhausted and with more of a sense of relief than satisfaction.*
>
> *At some point he realized that he was wearing himself out. The best reason to do any task, he decided, was because he wanted it done, not because of the pressure. He determined to change his habit.*
>
> *Facing a project at work that was not due for two weeks, he thought about starting early. He pictured the project completed a few days ahead of the deadline without him having to stay up all night to finish it. He imagined the satisfaction he would have.*

As soon as he started working on it, he noticed the desire to slack off. He could feel himself reverting to the old habit of procrastinating. When that happened, he deliberately recalled the visual image of himself calmly turning in the work early, and smiled. In time and with practice, the voice of procrastination faded almost completely away. George was able to finish work and personal activities with much less stress. His family especially appreciated the change in him.

> "A belief is not merely an idea the mind possesses; it is an idea that possesses the mind."
> – ROBERT OXTON BOLTON, playwright

Judgments, conclusions and beliefs. Judgments, conclusions and beliefs are what we hold in our minds to be true. They make up the building blocks of how we understand reality. The result of decisions we once made based on what we saw and heard, they bring order and comfort, and stabilize our understanding of the life we inhabit.

Most of the time our judgments, conclusions, and beliefs, like our habits, serve us well by organizing complex daily life. Occasionally, poor judgments, mistaken conclusions, and erroneous beliefs lead us down the wrong path and undermine our ability to understand what is really going on.

When Franco was a little boy, his extended Italian family would get together for holidays and celebrations. Franco especially enjoyed his grandparents and members of their generation who would speak together exclusively in the language of their youth back in Europe. Franco concluded that when you get old, two things happen: your hair turns gray and you start to speak Italian.

Franco's conclusion was perfectly reasonable based on his experience. How many of our conclusions and beliefs might be off the mark for a similar reason?

Like bad habits, certain judgments, conclusions and beliefs make life more of a struggle. And like habits, they came from emotional decisions in our past that made sense at the time.

Larry is an assertive person. He generally stands up for what he wants and usually gets his way. When he doesn't, he is quick to explain his failure as being someone else's fault: somebody "screwed him over".

At these moments, Larry is a victim and someone is to blame. He feels sorry for himself and is eager to share his complaint with anyone who will listen. He never concludes that he was not wise enough or persistent enough, or that he did a poor job. He cannot acknowledge that in life sometimes things don't work out. He is happy to take full credit when everything goes his way but unable to shoulder any responsibility when it doesn't.

How did Larry develop such an attitude? Most likely it grew up from something that happened once, when he didn't get what he wanted and decided to blame someone else. Blaming was easier than feeling incompetent. Perhaps he learned to see himself as a victim from his parents. Wherever it came from, Larry carries around a repeating victim story that he trots out whenever anything doesn't work out right. It does not occur to him that victimhood is his judgment and not necessarily an accurate picture of reality.

> If you can start to see these conclusions and beliefs not as reality but as opinions, you might be able to revise them in the face of new knowledge and experience.

Judgments, conclusions and beliefs are hard to shake loose because we perceive them as facts and see them from our own point of view: it's hard to get a new perspective on our own thinking from inside that thinking. Many people carry around secret beliefs that make life harder: "There is never enough time." "I am not worthy of being loved." "I'm too young or too old or not rich enough to do what I want to do."

If you can start to see these conclusions and beliefs not as reality but as opinions—even opinions for which you have a lot of evidence—you might be able to revise them in the face of new knowledge and experience. Imagine each of these, or your own personal conclusions or beliefs, preceded by the words, "I believe that..." or "I am of the opinion that..." Notice how different that feels. How might Larry's life be different if he could learn to say, "I have an opinion that I've been screwed"?

Recognizing judgments, conclusions, and beliefs for what they really are, instead of mislabeling them as "the truth" or "reality," is a powerful step toward being able to acknowledge honest feelings. It starts with asking the simple question, "How do I feel?" and listening to the answer.

Try this: Find an assumption or belief that you have that makes your life more difficult. Typical examples include "I never have enough money" or "People don't understand/respect me." Restate that belief as, "I used to think that..." Repeat this to yourself for a while and watch how your relationship with this issue changes.

Summary

- We often fail to recognize uncomfortable feelings for what they are.
- The frank and honest understanding of current emotions helps us to move through confusing or difficult feelings.
- Emotional authenticity makes for healthy relationships and effective communication.
- A generally positive outlook, based in emotional truthfulness, lifts our spirits and encourages us to move forward.

CHAPTER 5

Moving On

The most powerful moment in life is this moment, right now. Only in this moment can we make choices and take action. For our emotional system to be healthy and resilient, it must stay in touch with, and engaged with, the present. Time and life move only in one direction: forward. And so must we.

This is not to diminish the importance of the past or minimize its influence. We can learn from our past. But we cannot afford to get stuck there, replaying a script whose time has passed and that no longer serves us.

However significant it was at the time, the past is over. Feelings based on what we remember or imagine from the

> "In three words I can sum up everything I've learned about life: it goes on."
> – ROBERT FROST, poet

past are *today's* feelings. However they influence what we think and do, they are the emotions of *right now*. When we honor our personal history— the parts we like and the parts we don't—and turn our attention forward, we can begin to move on.

Personal narratives and moving on

Everyone has a personal narrative. Much has happened in our lives, but we don't remember every incident equally well. What sticks in memory are the events that are linked to strong emotion.

Great joys and sadness, moments of stark fear or exquisite love, experiences of pride or humiliation stay with us. Our most important achievements are memorable not for the events themselves but for the emotions they evoked. We remember the details of a great sports victory not because our team won, but because we felt so excited about it. Similarly, most Americans remember exactly where they were when they heard about the assassination of President Kennedy or the 9/11 attacks.

> However significant it was at the time, the past is over.

These memories are meaningful as touchstones of our personal history. But the past does not determine the future. Our past provides a foundation upon which we can build a future of our own design.

Alison and her sister sounded almost exactly alike when they were teenagers. Once, as a joke, Alison answered a boy's call pretending to be her sister. Her father overheard the conversation.

When Alison hung up, her father said, "You're as crooked as a dog's hind leg."

Alison was deeply wounded by her father's comment. Losing the trust of her normally loving father hurt her deeply. She began to question her own honesty and integrity. What started as a simple prank between sisters raised questions about her own worthiness. Years after her father had forgotten the incident, Alison carried around feelings of self-doubt because of her dad's one-time remark.

Your personal narrative has stories from childhood like Alison's that seemed important at the time, even if they amount to little now. What conclusions did you make from them? How have those conclusions shaped your self image? What happened years ago that limits your potential now?

The point is not to sort through your past: it's to honor the past and let it go. Even powerful events from the past can only continue to hurt you if you let them.

> "Nothing ever happened in the past; it happened in the Now. Nothing will ever happen in the future; it will happen in the Now."
> – ECKHART TOLLE, spiritual teacher

It may help to write your autobiography, keep a journal or explore your emotional past more deeply with professional help. Reviewing your personal narrative offers insight into how you got to be the way you are. It provides an opportunity to choose how you want to move forward.

> *A journalist interviewing playwright Arthur Miller brought up the subject of Marilyn Monroe, the famous actress to whom Miller had been married decades earlier. Monroe, the biggest star and sex symbol of her era, was a troubled woman who ended her life in suicide. The journalist was looking for some spicy gossip to fill out his interview.*
>
> *Miller was too wise to be caught up in the sensationalism of the past. After divorcing Monroe, he moved on. He told the journalist that there was nothing left to say about that part of his past. He wasn't angry about being asked, he just knew that that chapter of his life was over. He was not willing to indulge in old stories and completed emotions just because a journalist asked him to.*

Miller's attitude was positive and healthy: "Next!" He had made his peace with that part of his history and had the emotional resilience to turn his attention forward.

We naturally use the past and its lessons to help us navigate the present.

> *Doug went to an investment advisor with his portfolio of stocks, bonds and cash. The advisor looked over the portfolio and asked, "If we were starting from scratch today, where should we be investing your assets?"*

Doug realized that some of the stocks he owned had been in his portfolio for a long time. He had a sentimental attachment to them. Some he kept because they had been successful and he could look proudly at how much they had grown. Others were down, and he was waiting for them to make back the losses before selling.

His advisor patiently told Doug that none of that history or emotional attachment mattered if the purpose of his investments was to grow in value. Doug heard him. He felt a little sad about dumping old stocks, but he understood that a portfolio based on today's needs and today's market conditions made a lot more sense.

Your life story is unfinished. You have an idea how you want the rest of it to turn out. Consider the joys and disappointments that got you to where you are today as pages in a history book, learn from them, and look forward.

Newness

Human beings are programmed to embrace novelty. We are attracted to the newest gadgets, cars, and strategies for managing our lives and our businesses. We imagine that new ways of doing things are better and will make us happier. Commercial messages are created to pique our interest in all manner of new products and ideas. We may

LOCUS OF CONTROL

The psychological concept of the Locus of Control, originally developed by Julian B. Rotter, has to do with a person's level of belief about the causes of what happens to them. Internal locus of control people believe that they are the source of most of what happens. Through their own initiative, decisions and actions, they believe that they bring upon themselves good or bad results. External locus of control people are more likely to perceive outside influences such as luck and the actions of others as determining what happens in their lives. Not surprisingly, research suggests that high internal locus of control people—who feel responsible for their own lives—are more successful and confident than those at the other end of the spectrum.

Locus of control orientation is influenced by genetic predisposition and upbringing, but can also be affected by personal choice, habit, and learned behavior. High "internals" are more likely to come from families where parents modeled similar behavior and gave their children more responsibility for the consequences of their actions. Socioeconomic class is a factor as well, as lower income people tend to see their plight as being due to circumstances over which they never had control.

know in our hearts that new products won't increase happiness for more than a short time, but most of us still can't help being attracted to that which is new.

Emotions are *always* new. Since emotions exist only in the current moment, each feeling is fresh and new every time. There are only so many kinds of emotions: the feelings we feel at any given time may be familiar. Familiar or not, each emotional state is born anew every time.

Romance stories from *Romeo and Juliet* to *Slumdog Millionaire* follow a reliable formula. The lovers meet, are attracted to one another, and struggle to resolve obstacles. If the story has a happy ending, they end up together, in love. If it's a tragedy, they end up apart or dead. If the stories are well told, the audience is uplifted by the happy endings and moved by the tragic ones.

> "Change is the watchword of progression. When we tire of well-worn ways, we seek for new. This restless craving in the souls of men spurs them to climb, and to seek the mountain view."
> – ELLA WHEELER WILCOX, poet

The plot line is predictable. Why do we enjoy them time after time? Because even though the story may be old, our emotional response is always new. We are moved every time by Humphrey Bogart's character's nobility in *Casablanca* and uplifted by the love between Maria and the Baron in *The Sound of Music*. In the same way, feelings of affection for a spouse or friend or child do not get old from one day to the next because the emotions themselves are always fresh in the moment.

As we come to understand our emotions and strive to enhance our emotional health, newness on the outside means little, but newness on the inside means everything. Staying connected to the new feelings of *this moment right now* is critical to feeling alive and engaged.

Try this: When you hear a news story about a brand new gadget or piece of software, notice how fascinating it appears simply because it's new. Recognize that its newness, at least at first, adds to its appeal.

Summary

- Emotions exist in the present moment only, though they may be related to considerations of the past or future.
- Staying emotionally in touch with the current moment helps us to move forward.
- We may need to recount stories from our past so we can complete them and turn our attention to the present.

CHAPTER 6

The Circle of Emotions

All human emotion naturally falls into two categories: pleasant, enjoyable feelings and difficult, painful or uncomfortable ones. The two categories of emotions might seem like opposites, but there is no conflict. Each category is a complementary aspect of the larger whole: the emotional system. Each is a feeling response to the presence or absence of Oneness.

An all-encompassing circle

We can depict the complementary nature of the two categories of emotions with a version of the traditional Taoist circle of yin and yang. This symbol emphasizes that the two sides are inter-related components of the same whole.

73

To look at this ancient symbol is to see all the primary emotions as interconnected journeys rather than separate events. Moment-to-moment feelings are not fixed, but move continually within the Circle. Feelings shift from one side of the Circle to the other, as when a moment of sadness is transformed by the touch of love. They also move more subtly within a single emotion, as through the many faces of grief or the variations on pleasure. No matter how unpredictably feelings shift, no emotional experience exists in isolation.

Similar feelings, different feelings

On the pleasurable side of the Circle, love, feelings of social connectedness, and happiness, share a theme of relationship and connection. As expressions of Oneness they all feel good. On the other side of the Circle, emotions representing the absence of connection feel quite different from one another. Sadness and grief feel very different from anger and hatred, and fear is something else entirely.

Unpleasant emotions feel so different from one another because each is a strategy to address a different aspect of the absence of Oneness. When we feel the loss of connection, our emotional system springs into action to restore balance. Sometimes that means feeling sad or grieving through a loss. At other times a more aggressive approach—getting angry—is called for. Fear prepares us to face what might happen in the future. There are also times when the system is so overloaded that it simply needs to rest and recover. At these times we may feel beaten down, or just plain tired.

> "There are as many nights as days, and the one is just as long as the other in the year's course. Even a happy life cannot be without a measure of darkness, and the word 'happy' would lose its meaning if it were not balanced by sadness."
> – CARL JUNG, psychologist

If we fail to understand the interrelated nature of emotion, it would be easy to think in terms of either/or, as if the different emotions were in some kind of conflict. When we appreciate the Circle of Emotion, it becomes clear that all the parts are working together in an integrated system. Once we begin noticing how the system works, our emotional life becomes more transparent, and the journey becomes more manageable.

Trusting the circle

Coming to understand the interrelated nature of all emotion unlocks an important pathway to emotional health.

> The reason the unpleasant emotions each feel so different is that each is a strategy to address a different aspect of the absence of Oneness.

I majored in psychology in college. Then as now, I was fascinated with trying to understand why people behave the way they do. So it was especially frustrating that even with all my learning and study, my own emotions felt unreliable well into my late 20's. I used to stumble between laughter and the verge of tears unpredictably. I would have dinner with a friend or go out on a good date and feel that everything was wonderful, then wake up the next morning despondent. It was painful.

I thought I should be past what seemed like all that adolescent stuff, but this thought only made me feel worse. Because I did not know any better, I imagined that how I felt was the true indicator of how my life was going. The roller-coaster ride I was on—my own unpredictable mood swings—felt so unstable that it made me mistrust all my feelings and try, futilely, to avoid feeling much at all.

It did not work, of course. Roller-coasters can't start to go up until they have gone all the way down. I was struggling to keep the roller coaster from going down further to protect myself from feeling worse. The strategy was doomed. All I managed to do was freeze my feelings in a downward place in the cycle. I eventually learned an important lesson: The sooner we reach the bottom, the sooner we can start to move back upwards and feel better.

At the time I didn't realize any of this. I wrongly concluded that feelings were either random and isolated, or completely out of my control, which was scary. I saw myself as the victim of each temporary emotional state.

I could not know, then, that I was the source of all these changes, not their victim. Emotions are not random. They are part of a life-support system, the emotional system, that is always on and always functioning.

> Emotions are not random. They are part of a life-support system, the emotional system, that is always on and always functioning.

Once you understand that all emotional shifts are transitions within the larger system you need not get caught up, as I did, in the uncertainty of what rapidly changing emotions mean. They don't mean anything beyond the current moment. Seeing emotions in a larger context, helps us begin to trust that the pieces all fit together, whether or not any given transition feels good or seems to make sense at the time.

Carl went to pick up his girlfriend at 7:30, having forgotten that he had said he'd be there at 8:00. As he drove up to her apartment, he saw his former roommate leaving her door. The friend noticed Carl and guiltily confessed that he had been seeing the woman on the sly for several months. Carl was stunned. Betrayal by two people he trusted made Carl sick to his stomach.

Back home, even while he suffered the pain of rejection and betrayal, a voice in his head that knew about the interrelated nature of emotions told him his suffering, however painful, was temporary. The former roommate hadn't been a particularly close friend, and the girlfriend wasn't the only fish in the sea.

Knowing he could not stop or change how he felt in that moment, Carl gave up trying to control his feelings. He let his emotions take him wherever they would, which included some dark, uncomfortable places. He could afford to do this because he knew that his feelings of rejection and betrayal would pass. Before too long he would return to his normal emotional balance which included the happier side of the Circle.

> **The Circle offers us perspective on even the most powerful short-term feelings.**

Carl saved himself more suffering by seeing the larger picture of his emotional life even while he struggled to get over a shock. The certainty that he would eventually be all right gave him the freedom to let his roller coaster hit bottom. It was painful, but only for a while and he emerged without scars on the other side.

The Circle offers us perspective on even the most powerful short-term feelings. During tough times we can gently remind ourselves that no feeling is permanent. With a little practice, we might even learn to navigate, by conscious choice, the journey across the Circle of Emotions back to the Oneness feelings we desire and enjoy.

CYCLES AND CIRCLES

The model of cycles and circles is widely used to help us understand all sorts of larger systems, including religion, Nature, even time itself. This model is ancient and enduring

Our calendar is cyclical, with twelve months corresponding to the earth's 365 1/4 day annual passage around the sun. Other calendars divide the year up differently for the same purpose. The Mayan calendar used in Mesoamerica hundreds of years ago featured overlapping circles of time.

Seasons turn predictably, day passes into night and back again, human life proceeds on a reliable path from birth and childhood to old age and death. Many people believe in an even larger circle of human life through reincarnation. Cycles provide continuity, and give us a sense of security. The biblical book of Ecclesiastes contains a poetic appreciation of the cyclical nature of existence:

> To everything there is a season, a time for every purpose under heaven. A time to be born and a time to die; a time to plant and a time to uproot that which is planted; a time to kill and a time to heal ... a time to weep and a time to laugh ... *Is it really surprising that emotions, so central to being human, should operate cyclically as well?*

Try this: As you interact with a few people today, identify where each one is on the Circle of Emotion. Notice what happens when that person's mood changes, and how those changes correspond to movements within the Circle.

Summary

- All emotion can be depicted as a circle with two sides, pleasurable emotions on one side and uncomfortable ones on the other.
- Understood in the context of the Circle, shifting feelings can be seen as transitions within a limited set of emotional possibilities.

CHAPTER 7

Feeling Follows Attention

Feelings can change rapidly. Since the contents of our lives usually doesn't change significantly from instant to instant, what accounts for sudden shifts in our emotional state?

The answer is to be found in *attention*, what we are noticing or thinking about right now. Our emotional state at any given moment reflects our experience of Oneness or its absence, as directed by our attention in this present moment. Feeling follows attention. How we feel right now is bound to what we are perceiving through our senses or thinking about at this moment.

It's all about attention

People are built to have their conscious attention on only one thing at a time. You can't read a book and carry on a conversation simultaneously. We might pay attention to a single subject for a while or jump from one subject to another. When we do, our feelings follow.

Michelle is focused on watching the latest episode of her favorite TV program. The telephone rings. She hears it as a distraction and feels annoyed. Annoyance is a mild variation on anger. When the caller turns out to be Joyce, an old friend she hasn't spoken to in years, Michelle feels affection, a form of love. When they talk about Joyce's new baby, Michelle feels joy and delight. When Joyce mentions a mutual friend who died, Michelle feels sad.

Had the caller been a bill collector, Michelle might have felt fear or even hatred. All these transitions, and so many more during the course of a day, are driven by changes in what Michelle is paying attention to.

> Our emotional state at any given moment reflects our experience of Oneness or its absence, as directed by our attention in this present moment.

At the moment her phone rings, Michelle can still love her husband, hate cold weather, and enjoy the taste of chocolate. But once her attention is on the call, her emotions of the moment fall into line with what she is paying attention to. If she were to think about her mother, Michelle's feelings about her mother might come forward. This is the normal, everyday way emotions shift and change.

Sometimes we deliberately manage our emotional state by intentionally directing our attention. We usually do this to escape or relieve an unpleasant feeling.

When our teenage daughter went out on her first date, my wife couldn't help feeling a little worried. Rather than fret away the entire evening, she put a romantic movie on the television and lost herself in watching it. Her feelings about this new stage of our daughter's life were still there, but the movie distracted her. As long as her attention was focused on the movie, she was able to put aside her worry. Had she not intentionally distracted herself, she would have been thinking all night long about how our daughter was doing.

> "Time cools, time clarifies; no mood can be maintained quite unaltered through the course of hours."
> — THOMAS MANN, author

It's hard to be thinking about personal problems while caught up in a thrilling movie or story. Many people turn to other distractions to manage uncomfortable feeings: going shopping, talking to friends or finding something sweet to eat. Those who turn to drugs or alcohol for relief usually end up creating far worse problems than the ones they are trying to avoid.

Sometimes we choose where to focus our attention on purpose; other times, thoughts just pop up in our heads. A song came on the radio yesterday that reminded me of a high school girlfriend. For that moment I thought about a woman who had not crossed my mind in ages. Feelings about her arose and passed in a few seconds. It seems remarkable that an old song could steal my attention and call up an old feeling, but emotions work that way. Feelings are a critical component of our sensitivity to the environment, since feelings guide us to interpret what happens and how to respond, and play a powerful role in the creation and retention of memories.

> "The trick is in what one emphasizes. We either make ourselves miserable, or we make ourselves happy.
> The amount of work is the same."
> – CARLOS CASTANEDA, anthropologist and author

Managing feelings through attention

Since feeling follows attention, we can often control how we feel on the basis of where we put our attention. Deliberately shifting attention to something that will generate happier emotions often works, at least temporarily.

We do this automatically all the time. Every time we plop down in front of the TV to take our mind off something that is upsetting us, we are intentionally shifting attention to manage our emotions.

While starting to fall asleep at night, I often imagine all sorts of awful scenarios taking place. In bed with the lights out, just as drowsiness sets in, my imagination goes wild with a picture of a family disaster or mysterious threat. I have no idea why this happens. But I have developed a solution. As soon as the thought occurs, before the accompanying emotion can upset me, I flick open my eyes. In the dark of the room I can make out the shape of a window, but that is all it takes to make the scary image vanish. After a few seconds I can close my eyes again. The dreadful thought rarely returns.

Moods, feeling states that endure for a while, can be hard to shake. A low mood settles in like a fog bank that can last for an uncomfortably long time. Occasionally it can be healing and restful. More often it feels like a weight that wears us out and offers no relief.

You might be able to lift a low mood by deliberately shifting attention to something you feel better about. Think of someone you care for or a good time you had recently, and let the feelings follow. If the low mood returns, as it often will, do it again.

An unhappy mood may require sorrowing, getting to the bottom of whatever is causing you to feel that way. But if the mood is temporary and not the result of a deeper concern, directing your attention elsewhere will help.

Don't let yourself get stuck in a low mood by thinking that just because you feel that way, it means something greater: temporary

PREOCCUPATION WITH SELF

A cartoon in the New Yorker shows a man on a barstool, talking to the bartender. The caption reads, "I'm nothing. But I'm all I can think about."

Preoccupation with self is a major cause of low moods and feelings of discouragement. The more we focus on ourselves and how we are doing, the harder it is to engage with others and our environment. People who obsess on their own emotional state never seem happy. Extreme self-absorption takes the form of narcissistic personality disorder, a threat to mental and emotional health.

In our happiest moments we rarely have any attention on ourselves at all. In happy moments we experience Oneness with the people and world around us and we are better off for it. During happy times with family or a lover, on a beautiful vacation or enjoying the arts, our attention is on them or it, not on ourselves. A quick way to break a low mood is to put attention on something outside that is appealing rather than our own lives and feelings. Volunteer work feels rewarding in part because it lets us feel good about ourselves without thinking about ourselves.

feelings don't necessarily mean anything. We can choose to feel differently, and we can use our attention to make that shift. Write in a journal, talk it out with a friend or therapist, throw yourself into work or go for a long walk. You have to find what works best. What matters is that you do something.

Attention grabbers

The focus of your attention may seem private to you. To those who want you to act in a way that benefits them, your attention is an asset to capture and control, with or without your consent. Advertisers are especially sophisticated at the attention-grabbing game. Because we are hard-wired through evolution to pay attention to loud noises, bright contrasting colors, rapidly changing scenes and the allure of sexuality, we are vulnerable to their techniques.

> "Feelings are much like waves: We can't stop them from coming, but we can choose which one to surf."
> – JONATAN MÅRTENSSON, author

A letter came the other day stamped "URGENT" in bright orange letters. As soon as I saw it my heartbeat quickened. It took only a second to realize this was a trick, a company's effort to get me to open an envelope and read a promotional message. I threw the piece of junk mail away. Even knowing well how attention grabbers operate, I could not help for a moment feeling my emotional system go on alert, simply in response to the word "urgent" printed in colorful block letters.

How many times have you seen a local fire as the lead story on the nightly news, even while major world events are taking place? Tragic stories, the sexual intrigues of celebrities and dramatic human suffering seem more "newsworthy" than happy events because they captivate attention. As they say in the news business, "If it bleeds, it leads." Violent shows and movies grab our attention and hijack our emotions in the same way. But is that what we really want to determine how we feel?

> Attention grabbers are emotion grabbers.

It is critical to learn to separate out the communications we care about from the onslaught of messages thrust at us every day. Only by filtering messages, the way a good email system filters spam, can we take control of the signals that have such a powerful impact on us. We also have to manage our natural responsiveness to new stimuli, especially as vested interests find newer and more clever ways to grab our attention.

Attention grabbers are emotion grabbers. In the end, where you put your attention has an enormous impact on how you feel. Despite the loud voices and beautiful people telling you what you *should* be interested in, only you know what you truly care about. Don't forget that you have a choice.

Try this: Notice how television commercials try to get your attention. What feelings are they trying to stimulate? Advertisers use fear, sex, humor, drama and the appeal of celebrities to capture attention. Without these tools, they can't transmit their message at all. Which ones cause the strongest reaction?

Summary

- Our feelings of the moment are influenced by where our attention is focused.
- We can often manage our emotional state by choosing where to put our attention.

CHAPTER 8

Love

At the heart of the emotional system is love. "Love" here refers to a deeply felt, enduring experience of Oneness, especially with a person. It can also apply to other treasured components of your life. Love is Oneness in its purest state.

People who have a lot of love in their lives—close personal relationships of all sorts—tend to be more content and live longer. Author W. Somerset Maugham, reflecting the philosophy of Plato, wrote: "The important thing (is) to love rather than to be loved." The act of loving others, much more than being loved by them, is what matters most.

Feelings of love are consistently stronger for some people than for others. Two factors that influence the strength of feelings of love are *commitment* and *momentum*.

> Two factors that influence the strength of feelings of love are *commitment* and *momentum*.

Commitment is the deliberate act of dedicating yourself to someone. It's what makes personal love feel personal. Commitment is the degree to which we invest ourselves emotionally in a relationship based on feelings of Oneness tempered by knowledge, values and other factors.

When we commit ourselves to a relationship with a specific man, woman or child, that relationship immediately becomes a powerful priority. Commitment is a decision to engage with someone dear to us, and to share life with that person in ways that fulfill the commitment. The other person's response matters, of course, but the act of loving commitment is ours first.

If it's a romantic relationship, commitment means we have chosen one person to share personal intimacy with to the exclusion of all others. Romantic relationships grow out of feelings of attraction and Oneness. Because we feel strongly about our beloved, we put other potential romantic interests out of the picture for as long as the commitment endures.

Other kinds of loving relationships are stronger or weaker based on commitment. Commitment to family and friends means that we go out of our way to involve ourselves with them. We care about what they care about. We willingly sacrifice lower priorities for the sake of those with whom we share this kind of loving commitment.

We may fly across the country to attend a friend's wedding. We may spend months or years looking after aging parents because our commitment to them makes their care important. Despite obstacles, we look for ways to maintain commitment with those who are close to us. Our willingness to support someone in times of need shows the strength of our commitment.

Typically, the most strongly committed relationship of all is that of parent to child. Parents are deeply committed to the safety, health and development of their children. Even once the children grow beyond needing parental care, most mothers and fathers stay devoted for life. Devoted parents say, "My kids come first," and they mean it.

Momentum refers to the strength of Oneness feelings through time. The longer a relationship endures favorably, the stronger the momentum. Months or years

> "When you make a commitment to a relationship, you invest your attention and energy in it more profoundly because you now experience ownership of that relationship."
> – BARBARA DE ANGELIS, author

of knowing someone deepen the quality of feeling about the person. Over time, that quality of feeling builds momentum and persists unless something happens to alter it.

A history of shared experiences enhances momentum. In 2004, Red Sox fans everywhere were thrilled when the team finally won their first World Series in 81 years. Those who had endured decades of spectacular failures and narrow misses felt especially connected with one another after so many years of shared frustration.

As the trunk of a tree thickens with the years, we naturally feel closer to those with whom we have been agreeably connected for a long time. That is why family feelings can be so powerful, even for relatives we see only rarely. Simply going through life for years and years increases the momentum of the relationship.

We can't sustain a personal relationship with someone for many years and *not* evolve some kind of feelings for them. Even happenstance relationships, with neighbors or coworkers, accumulate momentum. After a few months in close proximity, we feel affection or dislike for the woman in the next cubicle or the quirky old man who lives next door.

> We can't sustain a personal relationship with someone for many years and *not* evolve some kind of feelings for them.

At a college reunion a few years ago, I struck up a conversation with the one classmate who lives in my town. He and I had known of each other, but we had not talked in the decades since graduation. Despite different occupations and backgrounds, there was a feeling of affinity based solely on the momentum of our common experience.

Since then we have become friends. Without the college connection this would not have happened. The momentum of our shared history, though the connection was tenuous and happened long ago, generated a sympathetic feeling that eventually blossomed into a meaningful personal friendship.

Noticing commitment and momentum

Where do your personal relationships stand in terms of commitment and momentum? You can evaluate each one. The ones with the highest level of commitment that have also lasted a long time command the strongest, most enduring feelings of connection. Relationships with people you've met only recently or those long-standing ones with lower commitment tend to be less meaningful.

For teenagers, the rush of emotion in a first romance brings forth a flood of powerful feelings. Infatuation is glorious. The level of commitment—a strong feeling of attraction—is high, but the momentum is low. Unless they stay together over time, the romance disintegrates as quickly as it started.

Relationships with high momentum and low commitment feel less intimate.

> *When Vic moved his young family to the suburbs, he made sure to meet all his new neighbors. One was an older woman who lived by herself down the block. Though they rarely spoke after that, Vic waved to her and smiled whenever he saw her. Ten years later, when the woman passed away, Vic was surprised to feel so sad. His emotional bond with her, the feeling of closeness, had been based entirely on the momentum of living nearby for all those years.*

A matrix of individual relationships with high or low commitment and momentum would look like this:

Momentum

		Low	High
Commitment	High	New friends Romantic infatuation A spiritual leader	Parents Spouse Children Siblings Closest friends
	Low	Acquaintances The people you meet Business interactions	Neighbors Colleagues Long time casual friends Idols and public figures

Profound feelings of connection can happen with neither momentum or commitment. With no enduring power, they do not last.

I was stuck on an elevator for an hour once in a New York City apartment building with three women. One seemed particularly nervous. The rest of us quickly began to talk, even joke a little to settle her—and ourselves—down. Within a few minutes the conversation had become quite lively. We laughed together and a feeling of closeness grew.

Our only commitment to one another was based in the intuitive understanding that we shared a common fate: whatever happened to one of us was likely to happen to all. We were also physically very close together. We never formally introduced ourselves or found out each other's names until it was all over.

By the time we were rescued, we felt camaraderie and even affection for one another. But there was no relationship commitment. The time we spent together on that hot elevator might have seemed like an eternity, but it was barely an hour, not long enough to generate any momentum. No feelings for each other endured after we went our separate ways. A month later I probably would not have recognized any of them.

Relationships change over time. Acquaintances can become close friends, colleagues can become adversaries. Many relationships are so complex that they include a mix of both attractive and repulsive feelings, and the mix is subject to continual change.

Personal love

Personal love is a direct, individual emotional Oneness connection with another person. Romantic relationships are one example, but other intimate bonds may be even more important because there are more of them and they can last a lifetime.

The first Oneness connection we have is with our mother. If a newborn's helpless dependency does not at first look like what we think of as personal love, the mother's doting affection surely does. A new mom's adoration of her baby is bliss unparalleled.

As we grow up, our parents stay in personal love with us. Because the bond is secure, families are able to endure the inevitable disagreements and conflicts of adolescence. We know the love will be there when the struggle subsides. This is important since it allows young people a safe environment in which to try out new identities and develop their own characters. Family fights would take on a very different nature if a teenager thought an angry outburst could cause the parent to permanently abandon loving him or her.

Children begin to recognize their own capacity to feel love, especially for their parents, early on. Beyond the simple need to be cared for, we develop feelings of attachment and devotion. As we grow up, those feelings of closeness become part of our emotional repertoire. We come to love other family members and friends. As we mature, our capacity for feeling personal love becomes more diverse, leading to boyfriends and girlfriends and eventually lovers and mates.

> "Love is a force that connects us to every strand of the universe, an unconditional state that characterizes human nature, a form of knowledge that is always there for us if only we can open ourselves to it."
> – EMILY HILBURN SELL, author

We also develop strong bonds of friendship and dedication to teachers and mentors. We do not love these people in the same way we love a father or a sister, but the feelings of personal emotional connection can be just as strong.

It is possible to have direct personal love for many people at the same time. You can love—deeply and personally—your spouse, your child, your neighbor, your old friend from high school and your mother-in-law each in a distinct way. Each relationship has its own characteristics and nuances.

It has been said that the true success of a person's life can be measured by the quality of their long-term relationships.

> Those who have strong personal connections across a broad spectrum of relationships, bonds of Oneness that last over many years, are likely to be satisfied and content with their lives.

Those who have strong personal connections across a broad spectrum of relationships, bonds of Oneness that last over many years, are likely to be satisfied and content with their lives for a long time.

Transcendent love

We also experience personal love beyond the realm of personal relationships. Passionate feelings of devoted love for a treasured ideal or idea—transcendent love—can be just as powerful and committed as those directed toward people.

Transcendent love evokes a higher ideal. Love of Truth, Liberty, or Art can be a deeply held passion. Devotion to a Higher Power may be a feeling as powerful as any.

LOVE AND THE ARTS

Personal love, for all its richness and meaning, is awfully hard to put into words. We simply don't have effective language for describing what the feeling is like.

Instead, we have the arts. Books, movies, poetry and music help illuminate feelings that are hard to talk about, especially in the realm of romance. Artists and writers represent through their art what they cannot describe in ordinary language. We who enjoy their creations appreciate their effort because we can't pin down the words to express such powerful emotion either.

The Roman poet Catullus wrote about romantic love two thousand years ago. In the Middle Ages, Dante was inspired by his adoration of Beatrice. Flaubert's Madame Bovary is a story about the intensity of romantic desire, as are thousands of contemporary romance novels that sell millions of copies. In West Side Story, when Tony and Maria sing of their romantic love for one another, it touches us because their love is so strong. We recognize the magnificence of how they feel because we can feel it too.

Even the most fulfilling personal relationships can be frustrating and disappointing at times. Through the arts we get a taste of the romantic feelings of love and wholeness we long for without the complications of real life.

Transcendent love is similar to personal love but without another person as its object. The emotional commitment is deeply felt and typically has momentum that endures over many years. It may arrive unexpectedly as in a moment of revelation. Once a part of you, it is likely with you for life. Transcendent love shares other characteristics of any great love, such as a feeling of intimacy, belonging, and a sense of eternal connection.

> "Your words are my food, your breath my wine."
> – SARAH BERHNARDT, actress

The love of Nature can be a profound Oneness feeling. There are those who love their country so much that they are willing to risk their lives to defend it. Devotion to God is a common example of transcendent love.

Mac was eight years old when music first touched his soul. His mom took him to hear a string quartet, and he was hooked. Right then and there he decided to devote his life to making music. He played oboe as a child, then went on to learn everything he could about music. He read about the lives of composers and studied the characteristics of the different instruments. He devoted himself to learning about as many musical genres as possible.

Mac's love of music never wavered. Today he is a conductor who spends 80 to 100 hours per week leading four different orchestras. He is especially devoted to programming for children so that others can have a chance to discover music as he did. He requires little sleep and spends the wee hours after midnight at home working on his own compositions.

Mac's infectious love of music spills over when you talk to him. You can feel it. He is lucky to have found a way to turn the transcendent love that inspires his life into a successful career.

Transcendent love is every bit as important as personal love in determining how we spend our time. Transcendent love is purer and may be easier in that it avoids the inevitable conflicts of relationships with people. Objects of transcendent love cannot love us back as people do, and they cannot disappoint or betray us. Transcendent love gives rise to harmonious feelings over the long term that enrich our experience of living.

In times of loneliness or failure of personal relationships, our objects of transcendent love endure. They help us through times of sorrow. That is why so many people turn to religion to help them deal with grief.

For many, reconnecting with the object of transcendent love—Religion or Nature or Art—can heal hurt feelings and restore a lost sense of Oneness. A spiritual retreat, vacation in an unspoiled Natural setting, or visit to a museum helps us refresh and renew ourselves. The objects of our transcendent love are touchstones in times of chaos and important allies that help us stay sane through hard times.

Searching for love

We are love-seeking beings. The ability to love, to experience Oneness, and the need to love are inherent in our species.

If we don't currently have enough love in our life, there is hope. The capacity to love lives within us, even though it may have gotten covered up by disappointment. Feelings of Oneness that are our birthright are still fresh and alive inside, waiting to be awakened and shared.

If we are thirsty for love we cannot sit back and hope some person or situation will deliver it to us. On the other hand, if we seek out people and situations where our love can find full expression, we will have a much richer life. If we devote our life to finding appropriate ways to share the love that springs from within us, and if we inspire others to do the same, we may just find ourselves having a pretty wonderful time.

Try this: Think of a movie or a play that had a powerful emotional effect on you. Why did it move you so? What happened to the characters that evoked a piece of your hopes, dreams or personal history? How similar is the characters' experience to something you understand from your own life?

Summary

- Love is a deeply felt, enduring connection with another person.
- Commitment and momentum influence the strength of a bond of personal love.
- Deep love for an ideal or idea is equivalent to the feeling of love for a person.
- The capacity to love is an inherent part of being human.

CHAPTER 9

Social Connection

Not all Oneness feelings with other people are as profound as personal love. *Impersonal bonds* generate milder feelings of connection with casual and social acquaintances. They comprise the majority of human contact for most people and contribute mightily to our overall feeling of belonging.

Danielle works at the bakery where I frequently stop for coffee in the morning after taking my daughter to school. She recognizes me now and usually greets me warmly, though she does not know my name. As soon as I walk in she gets my coffee the way I like it. I enjoy the feeling that someone acknowledges me as an individual.

> Casual social connections comprise the majority of human contact for most people and contribute to our overall feeling of belonging.

Last year she told me one day that she was getting married the following weekend. I congratulated her and wished her well. A couple of weeks later, I asked about how she enjoyed her honeymoon. When she cut down to two days a week, I asked why and she explained that she was working two jobs and dividing her hours. I know nothing else about her. All she knows about me is that I come to the bakery only on school days and how I take my coffee.

Danielle and I have an impersonal social connection. When I think about it, I do have a feeling of rapport with her, but only in a modest way. I share a similar subtle bond of ordinary liking with the members of a nonprofit board I serve on and with my daughter's soccer coach. We are not really friends and may never become friends. We are colleagues in a defined area of daily life.

How many casual social relationships do you have? Probably hundreds. Possibly thousands. You share impersonal bonds with neighbors you barely know, childhood friends you haven't seen in years, your dentist and your son's best friend's mother. If you are open to it, you can also feel an impersonal bond, even for a short time, with a taxi driver, bank teller, or a skier you ride with on the chairlift.

If you and another person acknowledge one another, talk together, and share something in common even if it is on only one limited subject or for a short time, you have a social bond. Even those people we meet once qualify, if it's a sympathetic connection ("What a beautiful day we're having." "Yes, it sure is.") Though none of these social bonds stands out, collectively they are precious.

The importance of connection

Humans are social animals. We need interaction with other people. The worst punishment for our worst criminals is solitary confinement. Years ago, singer Barbra Streisand sang a hugely popular song about people who need people being the luckiest people in the world. The song is really about all of us.

The great majority of our relationships are impersonal simply because there are so many of them. One person can only have a limited number of close personal relationships (see sidebar below), but the potential for impersonal connections is unlimited. Cowboy humorist Will Rogers's famous comment, "I never met a man I didn't like" shows how one man could acknowledge the potential for a social connection with anyone. Being open to engaging with others at any level can lead to an enormous social network and a feeling of belonging.

The basis of interpersonal connection can be as simple as sharing the human condition. It happens when we recognize that each person we encounter is made of the same stuff, with the same essential nature and same kinds of feelings, hopes and dreams, as we are. We feel the difference between a post office clerk who greets us with a smile and asks how she can help and one who scowls as she sells us stamps. The transaction is the same but the emotional experience is not. Impersonal bonds matter.

Encountering the beggar boy in Kathmandu (mentioned in the Preface) was a profound Oneness experience for me on a purely emotional level, yet it was impersonal. It was shocking at the time to have had such a strong feeling. When I did, I learned a life-changing lesson: If *he* was so much like me, *so was everyone else.* If I could feel a sympathetic connection with him, in spite of our vast differences, I could feel that connection with anyone, anywhere, anytime.

Though the emotion of that moment was strong, the feeling was clearly impersonal. There was absolutely no commitment to a one-to-one relationship. I took no responsibility for alleviating his suffering beyond whatever coins I may have given him. He had no interest in me except for whatever money he could extract from me. It was simply a human connection. Why it happened that day I will never know.

In a busy life with hundreds of brief interactions every day, it is easy to forget that there is a human being like us inside everyone we encounter. Just as you appreciate being noticed for the individual you are, so do others. It is a pleasant feeling to enjoy someone else's company even in passing, and gratifying to know that the person you are talking to recognizes the bond of shared humanity with you.

Commitment

Emotional commitment is what distinguishes between personal and impersonal relationships: not just knowing someone, but caring for that person. Only when you care for and about the other person—have an emotional commitment—can the relationship become personal.

We looked at high-commitment personal relationships in the previous chapter. The low-commitment half of the momentum/commitment matrix looks like this:

Momentum

Low	High
Acquaintances The people you meet Business interactions	Neighbors Colleagues Long time casual friends Idols and public figures

These are the impersonal social bonds that occur every day: people we are friendly enough with, but whose personal lives touch us less. Our investment in the relationship is small. I was happy for Danielle at the bakery about her wedding and glad she had a good honeymoon, but it would have been inappropriate for me to pry into more personal matters.

Commitment in individual relationships requires mutual engagement to grow. Something has to come from both sides. We may feel strongly about celebrities or historic figures. Without some sort of direct interchange, even our most beloved idols are only iconic figures and the relationship remains impersonal.

Leaders occupy a special place in our awareness. Because what they do influences what happens in our lives, we share an investment in their choices and decisions. No matter how strongly we like or dislike our leaders, the relationship is impersonal.

President Bill Clinton was a master at making people feel personally connected to him in an impersonal situation. Those who had the chance to meet Clinton for half a minute at a public event would remark on how they felt the president's full attention: "It was as if I was the only person he cared about in the world at that moment." Clinton was a skilled politician doing his job. He had a knack for creating the illusion of mutuality that made a strictly impersonal relationship feel personal, even if only for a moment.

Vast numbers of Americans felt personally connected to Barack Obama the day he was inaugurated as president. As the new president, he evoked powerful emotion, representing hope for the future and to many a healing of past wounds. No matter how much some might have wanted to meet or even hug President Obama that day, their connection to him was impersonal because it was in one direction only. Without some direct interaction, no personal relationship could exist.

Impersonal bonds can evolve into personal relationships when they become mutual and acquire commitment. It is rarer for personal relationships to devolve into impersonal ones, as anyone who has tried to be "just friends" with a former lover knows.

Momentum and social bonding

Momentum is also a factor in impersonal relationships. The passage of time, continuing positive feeling and increased interaction strengthen impersonal bonds unless something happens to disrupt them.

In the Boston area, where I live, there was a wonderful radio show every Friday and Saturday night that played great blues music. The host was an engaging woman named Mae Cramer who seemed to know just about everything about the blues. She told colorful stories about old blues musicians, men with names like Pine Top Perkins and Lightning Slim. Her vast knowledge of and enthusiasm for the music made the blues lady's show something I looked forward to every week.

When the station announced that Mae Cramer had died of breast cancer, I felt quite sad. Though I had never met her, she was a part of my life in a small way. My impersonal connection with her had momentum born of years of listening to her show. When I hear blues on the radio on weekend nights, I still think of her.

An impersonal relationship with great momentum—someone you've known for a long time—may start to feel like a personal one. But without mutual emotional commitment, it remains impersonal.

111

SIZE OF INTERPERSONAL NETWORKS

How many close personal friends and relations can you have? The number is not limitless.

Evolutionary psychologist Robin Dunbar has determined that the upper limit of personal relationships is about 150. Through his studies of people and apes, he concluded that a brain of a given size can only process a certain amount of the social complexity necessary to maintain truly personal relations. That number in humans approaches 150, "Dunbar's number", though under normal circumstances the number is likely smaller.

Author Malcolm Gladwell, in The Tipping Point, writes, "...150 seems to represent the maximum number of individuals with whom we can have...the kind of relationship that goes with knowing who they are and how they relate to us." Evidence from such diverse groups as corporate teams, military units and even primitive tribes seems to confirm this upper limit of personal relationships.

Impersonal social relationships, however, are unlimited. Consider the idea of "six degrees of separation," the astonishing theory that any one person knows enough people who know enough other people to reach every other person on earth with

> only six levels of removal. For Dunbar's number and six degrees to both be true, it is evident how large and important our networks of impersonal social relationships must be.

Never having met the blues lady, I could not claim a relationship with her that was anything but impersonal, and of course she never knew I existed.

Social networks and their rewards

Over the course of a busy day, we rarely even notice most of our impersonal relationships. The interactions are fleeting, and the feelings are subtle. Yet, collectively, they generate the social networks that link us to larger communities and help us feel connected rather than alone. Whether we are naturally gregarious, nervous, confident or shy, all those interpersonal and impersonal connections permeate virtually everything we do.

> "It is definitely detrimental to the bond of friendship if one has too many friends."
> – KONRAD LORENZ, animal researcher and psychologist

Every business is about relationships. Whether a business sells things or provides services, good relations with customers and clients is essential. Would you continue to do business with a firm that didn't value a good relationship with you?

"Networking" is impersonal bond building. When we network we are looking to meet people who can help our personal life or career, or introduce us to others who will. The smart networker looks for common ground, some form of Oneness, as the basis for new and promising relationships.

> Even with people who seem as different as different can be, there is an essential human bond.

Think about how many people you have known in your life, and how one acquaintance led to another and eventually a social network. Through them we meet our best friends and those with whom we fall in love. Our network of impersonal relationships makes up the fabric of life.

Even with people who seem different as different can be, such as a beggar child halfway around the world, there is an essential human bond. Recognize that bond to enrich your life.

I once attended a social event where the then-Speaker of the U.S. House of Representatives, "Tip" O'Neill, was the guest of honor. The meeting took place at a men's social club in the neighborhood where Tip had grown up. Most of the men sitting at the three long tables where we had gathered were blue collar working people.

For an hour, Tip worked his way down each of the tables, addressing each man by name, one by one. In many cases, he remembered the man's occupation and his wife's name. He apologized to those few men whose names he could not recall.

The men in the room were enthralled. Being recognized personally by one of the most influential men in America meant the world to them. When Tip concluded the evening by saying "I'd still rather be a lamppost in North Cambridge than the most powerful man in the country," the room exploded in applause.

O'Neill made each of those men feel personally connected with him, and of course won their undying support each Election Day. O'Neill understood, from his many years in elective politics, how important seemingly fleeting social connections can be. He confirmed as much in his most memorable quote: "All politics is local."

> "All politics is local."
> – TIP O'NEILL

Try this: Make a mental list of everyone you know well enough to say hello to if you were to meet on the street. Imagine each of them knows the same number of other people. How vast is your network of people only one acquaintanceship away? Imagine how much poorer your life would be without these social connections.

Summary

- Social and impersonal bonds make up the majority of inter-personal relationships.
- Social networks and impersonal relationships make us feel connected with others and give us a sense of belonging.

CHAPTER 10

Happiness

Happiness seems simple. Most people would say they want to be happy and would like others to be happy too. "Happiness" includes a wide range of enjoyable emotional states: pleasure, satisfaction, joy, delight, and so on. We appreciate and enjoy the many flavors of happiness.

In the Circle of Emotions, happiness clearly belongs on the Oneness side. When we are happy we feel connected, in tune, in touch. We have the impression that we are at the right place at the right time.

> When we are happy, we tend not to look into the underlying cause or the dynamics. We simply enjoy it.

There is a sense of harmony, even if we're not sure exactly with what. When we are happy we tend not to look into the underlying cause or dynamics of the feeling. We simply enjoy it.

Happiness has been a focus of American life since at least July 4, 1776. Thomas Jefferson wrote in the Declaration of Independence that the pursuit of happiness was an inalienable right to which all people of this new nation were entitled. Jefferson was no fool: he never said we have a right to happiness itself, only the right to be free to pursue it.

Many people would say that the pursuit of happiness is what life is all about. When I was in my twenties and would tell my father what I was up to, he would respond, "Whatever makes you happy." Directly or indirectly, in the short or long term, the choices we make are supposed to support or enhance our happiness, now or in the future.

Happiness and the emotional system

We saw earlier how a healthy emotional system directs us continually toward harmony and balance. The emotional system's job is to maintain stability in emotions, as other body systems do in other areas. We might call this emotionally stable state contentment, equanimity or a feeling of well being, all of which are consistent with the idea of "happiness."

> Oneness is the goal of the emotional system, because a state of balance is the strongest emotional position from which to face whatever happens next.

Being all smiles and laughter is not the point here. Oneness is the goal of the emotional system because a state of balance is the strongest emotional position from which to face whatever happens next. Our most dependable and adaptable emotional state is confident, relaxed and aware: the feeling that we are in a state of harmony and all our mental and emotional resources are available.

Unfortunately, our emotional system is not always successful in its mission. Mistakes, unforeseen circumstances, and external influences throw us off balance. Sometimes we make errors, our plans fail, and we feel anything *but* relaxed and content. Even then, our emotional system urges us in the direction of restoring a feeling of balance and harmony. However badly we feel, some part of us is always at work to regenerate our sense of well being. When we're at an emotional low point, that's nice to know.

Sometimes we are torn between pursuing what will feel good now versus what will prove more satisfying in the long run.

Ned loves ice cream. As a star athlete in school, he enjoyed a big bowl of ice cream after meals and as a late night snack. However, as he got older and less physically active, he was no longer able to burn off the extra calories. He knew he had to cut back.

Ned could not bear the thought of giving up ice cream entirely. His solution was to have only one scoop a day, and to eat that scoop in silence with his eyes closed so as to relish every morsel and every moment. Within a few months he was back to an acceptable weight.

He still loves ice cream. By focusing on what would make him happier over the long term—feeling healthy and looking good—over the short term pleasure of eating his favorite treat,

Ned was able to overcome his craving of three scoops of instant gratification. He doesn't mind when others laugh at his silent ice cream ceremony since he knows what it has done for him.

Young children seek instant gratification because they cannot imagine beyond the present. Adults recognize that what feels good in the moment might not work in the long run. Instant gratification is not a bad thing. For the most part, delaying gratification is healthier, because it allows us to organize more of our life around what is most important.

Happiness: A state of being

Though loving makes us happy, happiness bears an important distinction from the other powerful Oneness emotion, love. Unlike love, which is an active verb, happiness is a state of being.

> Happiness is a *by-product*, the emotional consequence of Oneness in some area of life.

We don't *do* happy and we never fall into happiness. We get to be happy because of our thoughts, actions and what happens. That's because happiness is a *by-product*, the emotional consequence of Oneness in some area of life.

I was busy at work a few weeks ago when I noticed on my desk a newsletter from my daughter's school. On the back page, was an article about my daughter having scored the winning goal in a soccer game. It even had a picture of her. The newsletter made me feel happy. I read it several times to extract all the pleasure I could from it. I felt proud, loving, and happy for my daughter's success on the field, and happy, too, to be her father. Then I went back to work.

The moment of happiness that day was a by-product of a temporary sensation of Oneness with my daughter and my aspirations for her, triggered by seeing the newsletter. Of course, I love her just as much when I'm not thinking of her. Seeing her name and picture in print put attention on my relationship with her, and as we have seen, feelings followed attention.

As a state of being, the feeling of happiness is temporary and subject to where we have our attention. As much as we may be attracted to the romantic idea of permanence, as in, "...they lived happily ever after," life doesn't happen that way. It comes at us in bits and pieces, often unpredictably. The goal, then, is to find or create Oneness frequently rather than delude ourselves into believing that we could establish any kind of permanent state of happiness.

Even when we know what is likely to please us, we cannot determine precisely what will generate happy feelings. Life has too many surprises. Sometimes we are happiest when we feel in tune only with our inner being. Certainly there are unhappy times we would describe as feeling out of tune with ourselves. Events and circumstances we rarely think about can also bring pleasure. We like hitting every green light not because we focus on such things but because we enjoy having the ride be smooth and easy.

> *Rona, a surfer, has visited many beaches and ridden many kinds of waves. "You never know which wave will be the good one," she says. "You try to pick the right wave and ride it as well and as long as you can. Sometimes it works, sometimes it doesn't. Sometimes a good wave closes out on you, and there is nothing to do but paddle back out.*
>
> *"You have to find the right moment to catch the wave and know when the ride is finished. If you try to stay on a wave too long you end up on the sand."*

A surfer like Rona is looking to make the best out of an ever-changing situation. The challenge—and the fun—is in managing to stay up on moving water that is only vaguely predictable. Surfing is an often-used metaphor for adapting quickly to a rapid change. Being happy, like surfing, often means adapting constantly to whatever happens.

TEMPERAMENT

Why do some people appear to be generally cheerful, some quiet, others melancholy? Since ancient times thinkers have speculated on why people have different kinds of temperaments. Four different temperaments, based on the four classic elements, earth, air, fire and water, were seen as the basis for different personalities as far back as Ancient Greece in the writings of Hippocrates and Plato. Amazingly, this view persisted into the 19th century.

British anthropologist Sir Francis Galton (1822 - 1911) was the first to make a systematic investigation into behavior and heredity. In recent decades, psychologists, biologists and especially behavioral geneticists have devoted considerable study into the underpinnings of personality. The strongest influence appears to be genetics. Each of us is born with a basic personality type that changes little over the course of a lifetime. Stephen Pinker, writing in *The Blank Slate*, suggests that even the most dedicated parents have little influence on the personalities and temperaments of their children once they have given them their genes.

Traumatic events, the norms of the surrounding culture and who knows what other influences may shape our personalities, but the basis for general personality type and temperament is rooted in our genetic makeup. However much we might like it otherwise, we introverted types are not ever going to acquire the gregarious and outgoing personality of our extraverted friends.

Happiness triggers

The thing that happens that makes you feel good we call a *happiness trigger*. Being in love is a powerful happiness trigger. So is success in most anything we set out to do, or eating a favorite food, or going on a long-awaited vacation. We don't think much about happiness triggers, but each of us could identify certain events that, if they were to happen, would make us happy. For my teenage daughter, a snow day off from school is a happiness trigger because she gets to do what she really likes to do, sleep late.

> "A sure way to lose happiness, I found, is to want it at the expense of everything else."
> – BETTE DAVIS, actress

Each person has a unique set of happiness triggers. Dog lovers delight in coming home to the wet nose and eager tail wag of the puppy that has waited for them all day. Those who don't like dogs find a big wet doggie kiss revolting.

The one thing that can never trigger happiness is the desire to be happy. While we want to be happy—and everyone does—happiness itself is not a directly achievable goal because happiness, as we have seen, is a by-product of some experience of Oneness. No matter how hard you try, you cannot drive yourself to be happy. If this is not obvious, imagine trying to be happy. When that doesn't work, imagine trying harder!

The best advice for people who are trying to be happy is to give up.

You cannot make up happiness any more than you can make up being in love. This explains why so many people struggle and fail pursuing the wrong goal—happiness—instead of legitimate happiness triggers such as good relationships, rewarding activities and spiritual understanding.

Most of us could recite a list of our favorite happiness triggers. Food, sex, play, socializing and for many people work are what we know makes us happy. Happiness triggers can be quite specific, such as lying on a tropical beach, playing with the cat, or attending symphony concerts. Many happiness triggers have a built-in time limit: what makes us happy for an hour or a day would become boring if it continued for a long time. It is not unusual for a newly retired executive to get sick of playing golf every day after a few weeks. The places we visit on vacation seem so wonderful in part because we are only there for a short time.

One's arsenal of happiness triggers changes over time with age and shifting priorities. An amusement park ride that is thrilling at 16 could be nauseating at 60. Other happiness triggers persist. From the time I was a child I loved the taste of blueberries and I still do.[*]

As long as we stay open and try new things, we can discover new happiness triggers throughout life. This is in keeping with the idea of happiness as a pursuit rather than a right or a destination.

Norman went into business in his late teens and worked seven days a week to build his company. Only after he retired did he

---

[*] Though I "love" blueberries, it's clear that blueberries bring me happiness, not love. We often use the word "love" in this casual sense to refer to things that consistently make us feel happy.

discover he had a talent for art. In a sculpture class near his winter home in Florida he found great pleasure in shaping clay. For the rest of his life, as soon as he got to Florida each year he signed up for another sculpture class and devoted himself to it. He produced some very sophisticated artworks that impressed his friends and family and made him proud and happy.

Getting to happy (or at least happier) part A

In general, we feel happy when what is happening in our lives conforms to our aspirations of the moment. Each of us has an ever-changing internal barometer of how the world should be, what it would take to generate a happy feeling in the next moment. We don't recognize the contents of this inner image because we have not created it deliberately. We don't think about its details. But below the level of conscious thought each of us has a set of preferred outcomes, a version of how we would like every situation to turn out.

While we can't control the outside world or predict our own changing thoughts and moods, there are things we know. We want to have good relationships and be respected and loved. We want to be successful at what we attempt. When we can get the world around us to conform to our unspoken version of how it "should" be, we feel happy about it.

Then, in the next moment, everything can change. Our interests, relationships, the tasks that were so rewarding, lose their appeal or disappear. Without even noticing it, our unspoken version of how the world should be has shifted. Since we are creatures of habit, we may continue to pursue an image of happiness that no longer exists, which can lead to frustration, confusion or sadness.

One way to pursue happiness is to distinguish what you really want from what you used to want or what others are telling you you should want. Then pursue what matters most. This can be hard in the face of habits, obligations, social pressures, the desires of people around you, and prior commitments. It may require compromises and hard decisions. To the degree you can chase today's dreams irrespective of what you dreamed of yesterday, you will open yourself to becoming happier.

> One way to pursue happiness is to distinguish what you really want from what you used to want and what others are telling you you should want.

My accountant told me of a client of his (we'll call him Joe) whose pursuit of happiness in the form of wealth had led him to completely lose touch with reality. Joe, a man in his 70's, had some $60 million in cash in the bank. He never invested in stocks because he thought they were too risky. He was not particularly charitable because he was worried that he could not afford it. He continued to work not because he enjoyed working but to make sure he would have enough money.

Joe had been poor once, and he grew up seeing money as the key to security from the hardship he had endured. His drive to earn money had been wildly successful, but he never noticed. He was unable to acknowledge that he had more money than he could ever spend. My accountant told me Joe was an unhappy man.

I don't know what Joe really wanted, but it had stopped being money years ago. Once he decided that money was the answer, he went on automatic pilot and stayed there. However much money he made did not satisfy him, and he never stopped to reconsider what was important. He failed to understand one of life's great truisms: *you can never get enough of what you don't really want.* If you keep getting more of something—anything—and it consistently fails to satisfy, you are chasing the wrong thing.

> You can never get enough of what you don't really want.

Contrast Joe's story with Chuck's:

Chuck is brilliant. He was a Rhodes Scholar then excelled at Harvard Business School. He was one of the youngest-ever partners in a leading consulting firm and became an Internet pioneer during the boom of the late 1990's. He worked 70 - 100 hours per week building a company that survived the Internet crash. When he sold his share of the company for a great deal of money, he reinvested his profits conservatively and thought carefully about what he wanted to do.

His first priority was to enjoy the company of the family that he had been too busy for. He and his wife left southern California for Jackson, Wyoming, a place he loved. He began to devote his considerable talents to environmental causes. He stayed active in his children's lives throughout their teenage years.

The levels of happiness of Joe and Chuck are worlds apart. Joe chained himself to an outdated goal he had long ago reached. Chuck continued to rethink what he truly wanted, and took action based on authentic priorities. It made all the difference.

Getting to happy (or at least happier) part B

What happens in our lives is only part of what makes us happy. The other part, often more important, is what we tell ourselves about what happens.

Virtually everything that happens is subject to interpretation. How we see and understand events and circumstances, our optimism or pessimism, our mood, and what we've learned from previous experience affect how we judge or interpret any single situation.

Sam and his girlfriend hopped on a crowded city bus in Lima, Peru because it was cheaper than taking a taxi. A woman towards the back of the bus waved to them that there was an empty seat nearby. They were tired and gladly made their way back and sat down.

As soon as he sat down, something felt wrong. Sam reached to his pocket and discovered his wallet missing. He had been set up. While bumping through the crowd to get to his seat, a pickpocket working with the woman had snatched his wallet. The thieves were off the bus and gone by the time Sam realized what had happened.

At first Sam was devastated. Cash and credit cards were gone, and he felt personally violated. His girlfriend comforted him and reminded him that they were not hurt and things could be replaced. Sam made a quick decision: he determined to get more good out of this disaster than what it had cost him.

As he filed a police report and talked to credit card companies, Sam paid attention to everything around him. He learned about bureaucracy, the machismo of the police and the compassion of strangers. He gained a depth of understanding of a foreign culture he could not have gotten otherwise. He became a wiser traveler and learned how to protect himself against a variety of perils.

Had Sam seen himself only as a victim of thieves, his trip could have been ruined. He might have concluded that traveling was too dangerous and stopped going overseas altogether. He would certainly have been more miserable had he interpreted the theft only as a disaster instead of also seeing it as an opportunity.

Most everything that happens leaves at least some room for subjective interpretation. We can always find positives in hard times if we are determined to be happier and willing to make whatever effort is required.

Not every dark cloud contains an obvious silver lining, but most losses can lead to growth, learning, and a better future. It takes courage to look for the bright side of particularly painful losses, and times of sorrowing may need to be completed before the healing and growth can begin.

Jerry was a successful lawyer before he went into the hospital for what was supposed to be a routine operation. He woke up with no feeling from the neck down. As he lay in bed, unable to feel his fingers, legs and most of his body, he struggled to come to grips with what had happened. For months he endured a brutal physical therapy routine to learn all over again how to get around and take care of his most basic needs. He searched his soul every day to make sense of his new life.

The rehabilitation hospital gave him extraordinary care as he found the motivation to rebuild. When he emerged, he was so grateful that he resolved to repay their kindness. He used his network of contacts to create a charity golf tournament to benefit the hospital. Within ten years he had raised over two million dollars to help paralyzed men and women get back into a semblance of normal life.

Jerry learned to walk—haltingly—and refused to be pushed around in a wheelchair. He stumbled and sometimes fell, but always insisted on getting himself up again. His example taught countless people in that hospital how to get past their physical losses and live happier lives through changing their thinking.

Jerry's life might have turned out differently after his surgery. He might have interpreted his paralysis as meaning that he was now supposed to stay in his wheelchair and be taken care of. Jerry is one of the most inspiring men I've ever met, not because of the cards he was dealt but because of how he played the hand.

> "People are not disturbed by things but by the view they take of them"
> – EPICTETUS,
> Greek philosopher

Balance in an unbalanced world

We know intuitively that life is uncertain, and the trajectory of our lives becomes what we make of it. As the famous opening line of Scott Peck's book, *The Road Less Traveled* says, life is difficult. But circumstances do not control our ability to be happy. We do. If circumstances were responsible for our feelings, we would be powerless to change how we feel unless those circumstances changed first.

Making yourself a happier person requires giving up on some of life's drama. Our entertainment media require dramatic ups and downs, joys and tragedies mixed in with anger and fear to hold an audience's attention. But drama is a poor substitute for harmony and satisfaction.

It helps to find a reason to smile. An authentic smile actually can change your mood. The neurological association between smiling and happiness is so strong that putting on a genuine smile, even if we have to make the effort to find it, relaxes us and makes us feel better. It makes others more comfortable around us.

It also helps to look for something in common with people you might automatically dislike or want to avoid. They are much more similar to you than different. Hostility and fear decrease when you can acknowledge bonds of commonality and Oneness, even with those who initially put you off.

Recall that, since emotions shift so frequently, the experience of happiness is always a temporary state. Exercise your right to *pursue* happiness; just don't imagine you can capture it.

Try this: Next time you find yourself in a hurry or worried about something, put on a genuine smile. It won't solve a complicated problem, but it will change the way you feel, if only for a welcome moment.

Summary

- Happiness reflects a Oneness connection with some aspect of life.
- Happiness, in the sense of contentment and balance, is the strongest emotional position from which to face whatever happens.
- We can't achieve happiness directly by trying to be happy and we can't sustain happy feelings by willing them to stay.
- We can pursue greater happiness by aligning with what we care about and by interpreting events consistent with what makes us happy.

CHAPTER 11

Grief and Sadness

On the other side of the Circle of Emotion, opposite feelings of pleasure, lies power. Through unwelcome feelings and emotional suffering come the opportunity to learn, grow and shape our life.

When everything is terrific, we hardly notice how we are feeling. Only when we are less than happy, it seems, are we moved to reflect on our emotions. Down times are the fertile moments that make us look inside and learn about ourselves. Emotional lows motivate us to do the inner work that can lead to healing and understanding and set the stage for future growth. They empower us to find new meaning.

> "There is a sacredness in tears. They are not the mark of weakness, but of power."
> – WASHINGTON IRVING, author

As pleasant feelings reflect Oneness, grief and sadness are the emotional response to the *loss* of Oneness or the *absence* of it. We feel sad when we lose what we value. A beautiful weekend ends, a favorite piece of jewelry disappears, a close friend moves far away. Something with which we felt connected stops being there, and we feel the sadness of loss. Or perhaps we simply don't have what we want. We wish we could afford to buy a house instead of living in a small apartment, or we yearn to be in a personal relationship.

These emotions are, by definition, uncomfortable. We prefer to avoid feeling them at all, as our emotional system tries to protect us from misery. Only when sad feelings are so sharp that we can't escape them are we inclined to acknoweldge our sorrow.

Grief

Grief is the pure experience of loss. We use the word primarily after a dramatic loss, as when a loved one dies, but other strong feelings of painful loss are virtually the same.

Grief is an emotional crater, the most painful emotion of all. At its worst, as after a particularly difficult death, the bond of connection feels ripped away, and grief can be all-consuming. Deep grief devours us and feels as though it will never end. Like jumping into deep water, a grieving person wants to find the firm bottom that limits how far down he can go. Afraid of drowning in grief, he wants to touch that bottom and propel upward to safer, more bearable feelings. But profound grief feels bottomless. It can be terrifying when the emotional pain is so overwhelming that it feels like we will never recover

Deep grief feels awful. But coming to grips with grief is a pathway to emotional well-being. Because grief is the ultimate painful emotion, it is also the bedrock on which the rest of the emotional system stands. If we avoid feelings of grief— if we cannot face the bitter pain of loss—we curtail our capacity for experiencing the full range of our emotions. If we are unable or unwilling to pass through deep grief, the

> If we are unable or unwilling to pass through deep grief, the pendulum of our emotions swings in a narrower arc at both ends. Avoiding grief restricts our capacity to feel happiness and love.

pendulum of our emotions swings in a narrower arc at both ends. Avoiding grief restricts our capacity to feel happiness and love.

Sorrowing, as we saw earlier, is the act of processing painful feelings of loss on a purely emotional level. In sorrowing we find our way, in an emotional sense, into the core of hurt, pain and suffering. The deeper inside these feelings we can get, the more control we gain over our emotional life. The closer we dare venture to the center of painful feelings, the more completely we can pass through them.

Grieving through loss

No example of sorrowing is clearer or more easily understood than grieving after a death.

My mother's death was a terrible blow. Though she was in her 80's and had been ill, to finally lose her was devastating. I felt numb and wept from time to time for days. Moment to moment I did not know whether I would be able to talk fondly of her or find myself in pangs of suffering.

When other people asked how I was doing, I did not tell them that everything was OK and that I was really fine, because it wasn't and I wasn't. I had lost my only mother forever. As much as I could during those days, I practiced what I knew about sorrowing. I would sit quietly and delve into the darkest feelings of loss I could discover deep within me. Usually these efforts would last only a couple of moments before the feeling broke up and I could no longer concentrate on it. If I was feeling strong I would force myself to dig into the sensation again. It was difficult and exhausting. But I knew that embracing feelings of grief as fully as possible was the right thing to do.

Feelings of deep grief tend to arrive in waves. You never know when, out of nowhere, they are going to swamp you. Time and again in the weeks following my mom's death I'd be feeling perfectly OK, only to be caught by a sharp, painful wave of grief.

When that happened, I surrendered to the intense emotion and let it wash over me. I did not indulge my suffering or feel sorry for myself. I simply honored the moment and its emotion. There were times when I was busy with something else, when I had to suppress or postpone it. But whenever possible, I let the feelings be. I never tried to make it OK by telling myself or others that she had "gone to a better place," because the issue was not where she was but where I was.

Though I still miss my mom sometimes, my thoughts about her are always positive. My grieving for her was completed. Memories of her are rich and beautiful. When she appears in dreams I am always glad to see her.

Grieving after the death of a lost loved one is a process with which most people are familiar. It is the extreme example of sorrowing. The same model of sorrowing can be applied, in proportion, to processing smaller losses, little "griefs," that occur all the time.

The first step is honest recognition: "This is how I feel." It may be important to distinguish the emotion itself from whether or not it makes "sense" to feel that way. Feelings often do not make sense. Then put full attention on the sensation itself.

If possible, try to locate a place in your body associated with the feeling, as if it resides there. Feelings of loss often locate themselves in the chest or gut. Finding a physical body place as a seat of emotion helps focus on the emotion, making it easier to work with and easier to find again later.

Put attention on that place and allow the feelings and their process to unfold however they will. Notice whatever thoughts, sensations and impulses occur to you. Just let them be there; you don't have to do anything about them. Go as deep as you can for as long as you can manage. If you can find a sorrow point—the single moment most strongly associated with the emotion—go to it. Regular deep breathing helps. Treat yourself with kindness, the way you would treat anyone else going through the grieving process. When the sensation passes, let the grieving end.

All sorts of feelings of loss, sadness, disappointment, rejection and failure can be laid to rest this way. Each will be a little different. Some might be completely healed in a moment. Great losses can take years to heal and leave scars. A man I met recently said it took five difficult years to recover from his father's death. Some losses are so great, such as the death of a child, that people never completely recover.

> Processing loss through grieving—sorrowing—is something *we do*, not something that happens to us. It is a source of personal power because it heals deep wounds.

Processing loss through grieving—sorrowing—is something we *do*, not something that happens to us. It is a source of personal power because it heals deep wounds. Awful as it can feel, it is the single most effective remedy for emotional pain.

Grieving is by nature a private process. Whether we take comfort from those around us or not, the healing happens internally and individually.

Ordinary losses

The death of a loved one is the extreme example of grief. At the other end of the spectrum are small setbacks. These are the little failures and rejections that happen every day. Most are so slight we do not even notice them.

Everything that goes even the slightest bit wrong represents a failure of Oneness with our hopes and expectations. The boss looks at you the wrong way or speaks to you harshly, and you wonder what you did wrong. You get a parking ticket. These small disappointments barely register as losses. They represent a loss with respect to how you want life to be or with your self-image as a successful, reliable or honorable person.

> Telling the truth about how we feel is pivotal.

Most of the time the emotional system tends to minor losses before they upset us, often before we even notice them. But if the hurt lasts more than a few moments, some kind of emotional processing may help. Telling the truth about how we feel is pivotal. Being truthful about our feelings grounds us, guides us and marks the beginning of our recovery.

Nobody is trained in the skill of sorrowing. It is hard to recognize feelings of hurt that can come from any direction and hard to know what to do with them.

Clearing up inner garbage

As we saw in the chapter on sorrowing, processing hurt feelings releases them and keeps them from getting stuck inside as inner garbage. We don't need to carry them around or doubt ourselves on their account.

Everyone has inner garbage lurking inside, wounds of relationship and failure from childhood on. For these wounds time has stood still. Their powerful emotional charge remains. We want to discharge them and let them go.* A real benefit of learning to grieve for losses large and small is that the stuck feelings become unstuck and you will accumulate fewer new ones.

> "The walls we build around us to keep sadness out also keeps out the joy."
> – JIM ROHN, business philosopher

The alternative is denial. Many of us are quite successful at denying or disguising wounded feelings. When hurt happens, better to notice it and process it now so we can move on cleanly. The habit of emotional honesty deters the further buildup of inner emotional garbage.

---

* Psychotherapy works this way. The therapist helps the patient work back through memories and emotional triggers to losses that occurred earlier in life. The conversation helps discharge some of the energy locked up in old events. In time the network of inner garbage held in place by that charge breaks down and the patient emerges healthier.

Sadness

The heaviness of sadness is what we feel when life is not going right. We are disappointed or unsatisfied due to the absence of what we desire. A common indicator that we are feeling sad is a sigh.

Everyone endures such times. Everyone sometimes feels lonely for lack of the right relationships or discouraged when struggling at work or school or family life. Even if we can't point to a particular event or a specific loss, we feel blue. The feeling drains and discourages us.

Grief and sadness occupy essentially the same emotional landscape. In general, grief indicates sharper feelings associated with a particular loss. Sadness is an overall malaise that weighs upon the heart. Loss also causes sadness: there is little practical distinction between the two.

> Though we prefer not to feel them, sad feelings can be valuable. They make us slow down, look inside ourselves, and realign with what matters most.

We commonly distract ourselves from sad feelings by shifting attention to something more appealing. As often as not the strategy works, and those feelings of sadness or melancholy go away. Sometimes they linger and settle in our hearts. Sad feelings can be valuable because they remind us what we care about. Sadness makes us slow down, look inside ourselves and realign ourselves with what matters most.

When Candace was growing up, her mom used to tell her that the only thing to do when you get a lemon is to make lemonade. The message stuck.

When Candace was rejected by her first choice college, she was disappointed. After allowing herself to feel sad for a while, she turned her attention to another very good college that accepted her and began to plan her education there. After graduating, when she couldn't get a job in her field because of a weak economy, she hunted down a program that let her live in Europe for a year as a nanny. Taking care of three children in a foreign country had nothing to do with her academic degree, but she learned a great deal and had a wonderful time.

Whenever things didn't work out, Candace acknowledged her disappointment, usually with a sigh, then quickly turned her attention to how she could redirect the situation to her benefit. She got so in the habit of making lemonade that the disappointments and rejections started looking more like opportunities and less like lemons.

When distraction fails to lift the fog of sadness, make peace with it. Be truthful about how you feel without trying to fix it. Find a sorrow point if you can and use it as leverage. Sadness is not bad; it's just uncomfortable. Use the quiet mood of sadness to reorient yourself to what you truly care about so you can move forward when the sad mood lifts. Perhaps you can train yourself to be like Candace and seek out ways to make lemonade of every lemon.

SADNESS AND DEPRESSION

Sadness and depression are not the same, even though the words are sometimes used interchangeably. Depression is a clinical state of extended feelings of despair. It is a mood disorder that can affect men and women of any age who typically feel hopeless, helpless, and with little motivation to take action on their own behalf. For a diagnosis of depression, one typically must have these feelings for more than a few weeks. Depression can be very serious, last a long time and even lead to suicide.

Sadness is fundamentally different. It is typically a temporary state of low feelings, one that can often be traced to events in one's life. Everybody has periods of sadness which eventually lift.

People going through ordinary periods of sadness may describe themselves as depressed because that's the way we talk. In conversation it is more common to say "I feel depressed" than "I feel sad." The book, *The Loss of Sadness: How Psychiatry Transformed Normal Sorrow into Depressive Disorder* by Horwitz and Wakefield presents a discussion of and distinction between the two.

It is beyond the scope of this book to assess any one person's emotional condition. Treatment for depression includes counseling and psychotherapy, and may include medication. If you suspect you have an ongoing state of depression, it is best to seek medical help.

Long-term sadness

Isolated moments of sadness and loss are easier to negotiate than extended periods of low mood that last and last. Long term sadness makes it harder to take positive action because the feeling saps our strength and confidence.

There is no easy fix for sadness. Processing the feeling by sorrowing may help, even when we can't identify a reason for the emotion. Tell yourself the truth and get enough sleep. The love and support of people who care for you is especially valuable during extended sad times. For people whose temperament gravitates toward melancholy, extended periods of low emotion may simply be a fact of life.

Be careful what you tell yourself about how you feel. Remember that how we interpret what happens is often more significant than the actual events. Since most media messages present only happy people, those of us who feel differently might wonder if there is something wrong with us. There isn't. If you feel sad much of the time, don't assume that most others are relentlessly happy. Telling ourselves that sad times are temporary can be a first step in emerging from them.

Recovery

Recovery from loss and sadness is a great teacher and a powerful source of confidence. When we emerge from the depths of emotional suffering we are stronger for having made the journey. Having done it successfully once, we become less afraid of dark feelings and more resilient.

It has been said that pain and suffering teach great life lessons, but that is not quite true. Rather, it is *recovery* from pain and suffering that leads to understanding and imparts wisdom.

It has been said that pain and suffering teach great life lessons, but that is not quite true. Rather, it is *recovery* from pain and suffering that leads to understanding and imparts wisdom.

Try this: Breathing is a ready tool to help us with sad emotion. Sometimes, we can breathe away sad feelings in a full exhale, like a sigh. Some time when you're upset, imagine the feeling attached to your breath and exhale slowly and completely. Notice that breathing this way releases and relaxes some of the feeling.

Summary

- Grief is the pure emotional experience of loss.
- Normal living naturally involves many losses and failures that generate feelings of grief and sadness. The process of sorrowing for great losses or small ones varies only by degrees.

CHAPTER 12

Anger and Hatred

Unlike sadness and grief that are typically heavy, internal feelings, anger tends to be hot, narrowly focused and sometimes explosive.

Garrett was furious when Kim canceled their date at the last minute. Again. It was the third time she'd called to say her company was sending her to Chicago where Garrett lived, only to bail out just before she was due to arrive. She always apologized, though not sincerely enough for Garrett's taste. Kim was extremely attractive, and Garrett was willing to cut her slack, but three times in a row was just plain wrong, and Garrett was very angry.

The next time Kim called to say she was due to be sent to Chicago, Garrett wasn't sure what to expect. When she called a few days later to cancel again, Garrett blew up at her. He told her he was tired of being mistreated and let her know how irresponsible she had been. He accused her of lying to him and stringing him

149

along, and told her never to call him again. For days afterward Garrett couldn't stop thinking about her and being angry at her. He wondered why it was so hard to get her off his mind.

Anger arises from a sense of violation. It's always directed at someone or something: you can't be angry at no one in particular. We get angry at an individual who does us wrong, a group that opposes our interests, a business that mistreats us, the government, God or ourselves. Sometimes it is easy to understand why we are so angry, sometimes not. Our anger always has a target.

On the Circle of Emotion, anger is far from love. There is no feeling of connectedness to anyone when we are furiously angry or seething with resentment. If grief marks a loss of loving feelings, anger indicates that such feelings did not simply get lost but were ripped away by someone or something. Whoever or whatever "did it" to us becomes the source and object of our anger.

> "Of the Seven Deadly Sins, anger is possibly the most fun. To lick your wounds, to smack your lips over grievances...is a feast fit for a king. The chief drawback is that what you are wolfing down is yourself. The skeleton at the feast is you."
> – FREDERICK BUECHNER, theologian and author

Anger blocks feelings of Oneness. Just as we cannot keep our eyes open when sneezing, we cannot feel connections of love or happiness during strong anger. Rational thinking shuts down and irrational thinking—typically aggressive and vengeful—leaps up.

Powerful anger is scary when it is directed at us and can feel just as threatening when it is directed at someone else nearby. Scariest of all is when our own anger is so powerful that we cannot even control ourselves.

> If grief marks a loss of loving feelings, anger indicates that such feelings did not simply get lost but were ripped away by someone or something.

Anger does not always explode. Sometimes it builds slowly inside as the violation continues and we try to manage our emotions. In the story above, Garrett felt more and more angry each time Kim disappointed him. Eventually the accumulated anger caused him to lash out at her.

Victim of what?

When we are angry we feel victimized. Somebody or something has wrecked our life, at least for the moment. We feel emotional pain and have someone to blame. The all-consuming emotional arousal gets to be about him, or her, or it or them.

It could be the boss who overlooks us for a promotion, the boyfriend who dumps us, the umpire whose third strike call cost our team the game. We can be angry at the weather for washing away our day at the park or the deer that eats our garden vegetables, or the liberals or conservatives or corporate polluters or environmental groups for ruining the country. We can be angry at old age for taking away our vitality or angry at God when someone we care about dies. Something of value has been lost, and we think we know where the fault lies.

We also get angry at ourselves. We get mad at ourselves for mistakes of judgment or saying dumb things, when we fail to meet our own expectations or those of the people we care about.

> "Anger blows out the lamp of the mind."
> – CHARLES J. INGERSOLL, lawyer

Even on those days when we feel mad at the world and everyone in it, there has to be a perpetrator. It is impossible to be angry about everything all at once or nothing at all. The emotional system simply does not work that way.

An irrational force

Anger distorts thinking. We can't think clearly and reasonably when under the influence of angry feelings. The emotion is too strong and too irrational to be acted on right away, as most of us have had to learn the hard way.

Anger may start as a slow burn that builds over time. It might leak into other activities or color personal relationships. We remember people who have done us wrong, especially if we have never fully processed the injury or forgiven the perpetrator.

152

Meryl was upset when her eight-year old daughter was picked on by other kids in her dance class. She complained to one of the other moms who said she would talk to her daughter about the problem, but didn't. Ten years later when Meryl and the other woman worked on a civic project in their town, Meryl arranged to keep her interactions with the other woman to a minimum. She was still angry about what had happened a decade earlier. Meryl had no desire to dig up the past and talk it out. She resisted the woman's attempt to become friendlier and continued to think of the other woman, considered kind by others, as a bad person.

Without thinking about it, Meryl made a choice to hold onto her anger. She carried it for years as a grudge. An opportunity for greater harmony in her community was lost because she refused to simply let go of an emotion tied to an incident long ago.

The rush of hot angry emotion can feel pleasurable, even exhilarating: the physical arousal of strong anger is a powerful sensation. Most of us control our anger well enough to avoid acting violently or causing lasting harm. But in moments of sharp anger we may still act rashly and do dumb things.

I once saw two cars meet at the narrow entrance to a bank parking lot. Each driver thought he had gotten there first and had the right of way. They stopped bumper to bumper with neither willing to move. This went on for a few minutes. I went up to one driver and said to him, "You are right. You got there first. But since we're all stuck here, why don't you be the bigger man and back up a little to let him by." He grumbled and brushed me off. I went to the second driver and said the same thing. His response was the same.

There we sat, a parking lot full of cars unable to move while two men sat angrily, unable or unwilling to think clearly and solve the problem they had created. I watched the comedy unfold as they grew more and more embarrassed. After minutes of stalemate, one moved just a little. Then the other moved a tiny bit in the other direction. Eventually they both compromised enough so that we were all able to go on our way.

Angry thoughts seem to make perfect sense in the moment. The two men bumper to bumper in the parking lot felt justified that they were in the right, at least at first. It did not take long for them—or the rest of us—to realize how counterproductive their anger was.

> There is no personal power in anger, even if it *feels* like there is.

There is no personal power in anger, even if it *feels* like there is. You can't act wisely and create value when filled with rage. Only after the heat of the anger has cooled can productive decisions, choices and actions emerge. Most of us know this intuitively. Angry voices attract attention, but cool-headed thinkers are the ones who change the world for the better.

Passing through anger

The trajectory of anger typically surges quickly to its peak and almost as quickly begins to recede. The intensity of the feeling and accompanying bodily symptoms are too demanding to last very long. One challenge in managing ourselves through anger is that by the time we become aware enough to start to think about being upset, the force of the angry emotion is already past.

Once strong anger starts to subside, other considerations—interpretations of what happened and thoughts about how to respond—begin to enter our mind. Do we need to take immediate action? Are we better off just dropping the matter entirely? Because anger confuses thinking, it may be difficult to put the situation into its proper perspective, and there is no single standard for what constitutes acceptable social behavior when we feel angry.

Josh grew up in a home where his parents never expressed anger. Not once during his childhood did he hear his parents argue or yell. Without knowing it, Josh came to assume that raised voices meant something terrible could happen. Whenever he witnessed an argument among his friends, Josh automatically stepped in to try to settle everyone down.

His friend Noah, on the other hand, grew up in a family where people yelled all the time. Angry display was normal. He joked that when his mother said to him over the dinner table, "Noah, you are the worst son in the world and a curse on my life," it meant, "Please pass the milk."

When Josh and Noah disagree about something, Noah raises his voice while Josh does his best to calm the conversation down. Neither is more angry than the other. It's just a matter of upbringing.

Restoring equilibrium after moments of intense anger is a critical function of the emotional system. The drive to restore balance dampens the fury of rage. Whether we need to take further steps or we can just let the matter drop, the emotional system rescues us from the unsustainable intensity of the moment and helps us move forward.

> Anger focuses our attention on something we can't change. Whatever caused our state of upset is probably over.

Anger focuses our attention on something we can't change. Whatever caused our state of upset is probably over. Continuing to stay wrapped up in anger ties us to a past we cannot influence. We're better off getting past angry feelings quickly so we can turn our attention forward.

As always, start by being truthful. Many people deny their anger because they fear the power it can have over them. Those who grew up in families like Josh's, where anger was never expressed, and those who have learned how damaging anger can be, may have trouble even recognizing when they are angry.

When you feel angry, annoyed, irritated, ticked off or furious, acknowledge the emotion for what it is and name it: "I feel angry!" Telling yourself the truth about how you feel often breaks the momentum of the anger and starts to restore balance right away. By focusing on the emotion itself, rather than on the perpetrator, the sensation will begin to shift as feelings reorganize themselves around a changed focus of attention.

All of us feel victimized, at least occasionally, and get angry. Nobody enjoys the helpless feeling of being so angry as to be out of control. That's why it is important to develop a personal strategy for passing through anger quickly. A man I know channels and releases his anger by crumpling up a piece of paper and throwing it hard into the waste-basket. As soon as it lands, his anger evaporates. It works for him.

Anger can be a bridge we cross or a castle we live in. No matter how unfairly we have been treated, staying angry for longer than necessary costs much more than it is worth.

The habit of anger

Like smoking, anger can become a habit. And like smoking, it is hazardous to your health. Habits, as we have seen, are powerful life-shaping forces. People usually pick up an anger habit in childhood, perhaps to get attention, or in response to events or those around them without ever noticing it.

Habitually angry people find it difficult to control the familiar chain reaction from perceived violation to angry emotion to explosive release. Teenagers, whose emotional habits are still being formed, may easily slip into the anger habit as they try to wrest control of their own lives from parents and teachers.

At 14, Beth has been led to believe that she should be happy, slim and popular all the time. When something goes wrong and she does not know how to respond, she gets angry. She's mad at her parents, her school, the boy she likes, the boy who likes her, and the person who left an ambiguous comment on her Facebook page. Her blowups don't last long, but they take their toll on the people around her.

Beth has a one-dimensional response to failures of Oneness. Where others might feel sad, disappointed or ill at ease, Beth snarls and blames. Anger is habitual and feels familiar. Her father understands this and can often laugh off her outbursts as just a phase in his daughter's growing up. Sometimes her angry flare-ups get to him and undermine their otherwise strong relationship.

A teenager like Beth will eventually come to take more responsibility for her own life as she goes on to college and adulthood, and her feeling of powerlessness will recede. As she gets older she will probably realize that blowing up all the time doesn't work socially, and she will learn other ways.

Beth's short fuse, common among teenagers, would be socially disastrous for an adult interacting with other adults. If you tend to get angry easily at all kinds of slights, perhaps you have the habit of anger. If you're not sure, ask people around you. They will be able to tell you.

If you find yourself getting angry frequently, consider whether you have really been mistreated or are just acting out of habit. How else might you act? Angry people can always make the case for who did it to them and why they have a right to be angry. Is there a more effective way to respond?

Life is frequently unfair to you and everyone else. To begin to escape a longstanding anger habit, consider each situation as part of the ups and downs of everyday living instead of one more example

> "Habit is habit, and not to be thrown out of the window by any man, but coaxed downstairs a step at a time."
> – MARK TWAIN

of the world (or someone in particular) out to get you. Rarely are others out to get you: they are too wrapped up in their own lives, pursuing their own interests. Start to unwind an anger habit step by step when the feeling pops up. Becoming someone who *used to* have an anger habit is a worthwhile goal.

Inner rage

Occasionally we meet people whose anger has been pent up for years.

When Martha was young, she endured difficult losses. Her mother died when she was ten. Her twin sister, whom she adored, was killed in an accident when they were in their teens. Her father struggled with work, and the family moved frequently, leaving Martha feeling unsettled and unstable.

Martha was too young to fully grieve for her terrible losses. Instead, she concluded that life had been cruel to her. Resentment led to a deep, inner rage that settled inside. Martha has gone on to manage her life quite well. She is happily married and a good mother.

But every now and again, Martha's rage leaks out. It appears as carefully controlled verbal bitterness that shocks the people around her. The cruelty of her words seems out of character with the woman she appears to be most of the time.

Martha suppresses her inner rage well most of the time. Others are not so fortunate. Inner rage can be a time bomb that threatens dire consequences should it burst out the wrong way. Martha does not recognize she has a problem with anger. She knows she gets angry at times but who doesn't? Because she manages herself well most of the time, the social consequences of her rage are few. She may never confront the dark forces that lie buried inside.

Merle traces his inner rage to his relationship with his father who used to beat him. As a teenager he channeled his anger into sports, as boys often do. Rage and athletic talent drove him forward to football stardom, eventually as captain of his college team and a stint in the NFL.

"I was successful in football because I was the meanest, angriest guy out there," he says now. Later, as a high school coach, he brought the same aggressive attitude, screaming at his young players to drive them to play harder. He eventually became a trial attorney where he could litigate with all the fury he had once brought to football.

In his late 50's now, Merle has become a gentle soul. After losing his marriage he realized how much his anger was costing him. A combination of maturity, self-reflection and religion helped him tame the demons that plagued him and drove him so hard. He was wise enough to see how destructive his rage was and find a way to let it go. He can even talk about his father now with no residual bitterness.

> "Anger is a killing thing: it kills the man who angers, for each rage leaves him less than he had been before."
> – LOUIS L'AMOUR, novelist

Powerful anger that causes people to lose control of themselves is dangerous. If you become so angry that you are a threat to yourself or others, you should seek help. If cruel words or violent actions

ROAD RAGE

Road rage forced the California highway department to shut down a road under construction when drivers frustrated by slow-moving traffic took out their anger on highway crews. In Massachusetts, two drivers arguing from their cars pulled off the highway where one took out his crossbow and killed the other.

According to the AAA Foundation, at least 1500 people are killed each year and thousands injured as a result of aggressive driving. Men are more subject to road rage feelings than women (56% to 44 % in an AutoVantage survey) and young men are especially prone to it. What is it about being stuck in a car that causes normal people to explode and endanger others?

Psychologist Dr. Leon James of the University of Hawaii suggests that the isolation and physical constriction of sitting in a car lead us to focus too much on ourselves and ignore the communal aspects of traveling with others. Stress and frustration build without normal opportunities for release. Driving is our only daily activity where a moment's mistake could cost us our lives, which makes us quick to react to the potentially life-threatening erratic moves of others.

Road and Travel magazine reminds us that it takes two to turn a disagreement into a battle. If someone acts angry at you from the privacy of another car, the best response is to ignore them and stay away. If you find yourself getting disproportionately angry at other drivers, plan ahead what to do when you start to feel that way or get outside help to avoid falling into road rage.

sometimes escape your normal demeanor, you would be wise to uncover the silent fire that burns on the inside.

Constructive use of anger

Constructive change may arise *from* passionate anger, but not *during* it. Angry times are ill suited to making positive changes because the heat of the moment is simply too highly charged to allow us to think clearly. Important change born out of anger happens later, after the strong feeling itself has passed.

> Constructive change may arise *from* passionate anger, but not *during* it.

Ruby was mad at her math professor. He ignored her in class and spoke to her in a condescending manner. One of her friends told her that this professor had a history of taking his female students less seriously. Ruby determined to prove him wrong.

163

For the rest of the semester, Ruby immersed herself in her studies. She got help from a math major friend and studied extra hard for exams. When she earned an A in the class, she was immensely proud of what she had accomplished. The professor's bias hardly mattered any more. She saw him as childish, hardly worthy of her concern.

Being angry does not solve problems, but it can lead to solutions by signaling that something is off the mark. In this way, anger can serve as a barometer that tells us whether we are on the right track or if a correction is needed.

If you look in the mirror one day and get angry at yourself because of excess weight, your anger could motivate you to change your eating habits and begin exercising. Anger at being overweight could spur you to become slimmer and healthier. The changes in diet and physical activity would have to last long after the angry feeling had passed, and you would eventually need to shift the attention to staying at your ideal weight.

Anger can be a catalyst for social as well as personal change. Anger about social injustice during the Civil Rights Movement in this country advanced the cause of human rights. The outrage of protesters inspired the general public to demand that their legislators change the relevant laws.

Sometimes anger teaches us nothing. If you spill spaghetti sauce on your new clothes and get mad about it, you still have to clean the clothes.

Hatred

If anger is an emotional explosion in response to being victimized, hatred is the extended angry feeling that does not go away. People who hate are unable to let go of being upset at whomever or whatever did it to them. They hold onto the feeling, stoking the fires of their hatred to keep it alive. Eventually they build a convincing case for how they continue to feel.

Perhaps the original transgression was so great that it feels unforgivable. Or they perceive the injury as continuing through time so that their anger feels justified. As great love seems to take on a life of its own, powerful hatred acquires its own momentum and commitment.

Individual hatred arises out of an offense or violation (actual or perceived) or a series of them: a horrible person has destroyed an important part of my life and I cannot and will not forgive and move on. Once anger blossoms into hatred, it takes on its own life and may persist long after the circumstances that generated it have passed.

> "Hatred is settled anger."
> – CICERO

In the book and movie "A Clockwork Orange," a man is disabled by a violent young intruder who also murders his wife. Later on, through a dramatic plot twist, the wheelchair-bound victim finds the supposedly reformed villain captive in his home. In a chilling scene, he realizes that the man he has locked in an upstairs room is his wife's killer. Hatred consumes him and he punishes the murderer relentlessly.

165

Of course, in real life, hatred is not so neat and extracting revenge is not nearly as satisfying as the movie portrays.

Though a person who hates can always tell you why his hatred is justified, the feeling is fundamentally irrational. This is especially obvious in the case of group hatred based on race or ethnicity. No matter how convincingly you explain your feelings of hate, it is hard to enroll others who do not share your sense of violation.

Couples who break up after being in love can hate each other bitterly. When the investment of loving emotion turns sour because of perceived violation, hatred can arise from rejection and betrayal.

> *Lisa hates Tom. After being romantically involved for a year, when Tom sat Lisa down and said, "We need to talk," Lisa was sure he was about to propose to her. Instead, Tom told her the relationship was over and he was leaving.*
>
> *Lisa was devastated. She wondered how she could not have seen it coming. When she discovered Tom had lied to her and had been seeing another woman, her feeling of betrayal hardened into hatred. She came to hate Tom as passionately as she had loved him. She looked for every opportunity to say awful things about him to anyone who would listen.*
>
> *Lisa's hatred had little effect on Tom, but it emptied her of energy and hope and kept her from recovering from her loss for many months.*

A healthy emotional system will resist the kind of frozen anger that leads to hatred. Where reason, good sense and an orientation to the future prevail, there is no room for hating. People who are emotionally healthy refuse to devote vital energy to keeping hate alive. They look to learn from their experience, recover and move forward.

> A healthy emotional system will resist the kind of frozen anger that leads to hatred.

Group hatred is quite different from personal hatred because of it social component. *What would you call a force that turned strangers into allies and inspired deep, unifying passion? What kind of idea could make rich and poor band together, disregarding their opposing interests in service of a higher mission?*

Group hatred is a community activity. When one group hates another group, the emotion becomes a powerful organizing force, creating bonds of fellowship and devotion that can look an awful lot like love.

The organizing document of the terrorist group Hamas is dripping with hatred against Jews. The Hamas Covenant says Jews "are smitten with vileness wherever they are found." The document blames Jews for the French Revolution, the Communist revolution, both World Wars, exploiting and corrupting humanity with the help of their allies in Rotary Clubs and Lions Clubs, and so on. Regardless of whether or not you see their political cause as justified, the Hamas Covenant is an overwhelmingly hate-filled document. Yet it has the effect of unifying a community.

Examples of group hatred are easy to find in ethnic struggles around the world. The stories sound pretty much alike: they have abused us and mistreated us; we have put up with their mistreatment to the limits of human patience.

For people living under difficult conditions, a target for shared hatred can be a welcome thing. In their passionate hatred of the enemy, they establish bonds of commonality that might be impossible to achieve otherwise. It's the paradox of group hatred: it strengthens Oneness feelings within one community by bitterly rejecting another community. This can be seen as the emotional system doing its job, creating stronger bonds of attraction among people, even in such a bizarre way.

Hatred is a cancer. Cancer kills by overwhelming healthy body systems with useless cells until the organs or systems collapse and stop working. Hatred destroys the emotional life the same way. By drawing energy away from the normal flow of emotions, hatred narrows the ability to feel harmony and satisfaction and live a diverse and contented life.

> "Revenge has no more quenching effect on emotions than salt water has on thirst."
> – WALTER WECKLER, author

What is under the anger

Anger and hatred are passionate emotions in response to hurt from a violation, real or imagined. At the heart of every such violation, however, is loss.

Garrett suffered a loss to his relationship hopes and his self esteem when Kim stood him up repeatedly. Meryl's loss was a mother's dismay when her child was rejected by other children. Merle's loss was a father's love and support to which he should have been entitled.

In anger, we react to the perpetrator and rarely notice that the feeling of hurt

> "At the core of anger is a need that is not being fulfilled."
> – MARSHALL B. ROSENBERG, psychologist

involves a loss. What if we put attention on the loss itself? If we did so, we would find that the feeling would not be anger, but sadness or grief.

If we could lift up the edge of anger as if we were looking under the corner of a rug, there we would find sadness: feelings of hurt and loss. Eckhart Tolle says, "Where there is anger, there is always pain underneath." It might be impossible to notice during an angry outburst. Later on, in a cooler moment, as we come to understand the workings of our emotional system, feelings of sadness lurk in the background after hot anger has run its course.

Sadness is a painful emotion. It's often more comfortable in the moment to vent strong emotion as anger and blame someone. But sadness and even grief reside in a quiet place beneath the surface of outrage and angry explosion.

Kenny felt a gnawing flicker of irritation at his girlfriend Yolanda every time he came home after a date. He enjoyed her company and they had some lively times. But when they were apart he couldn't help feeling annoyed with her, though it didn't seem to make sense.

> If we could lift up the edge of anger as if we were looking under the corner of a rug, there we would find sadness.

One day his Mom asked how he was doing with Yolanda, and Kenny told her about being mad at her so much of the time.

His mother asked, "Is she treating you right?" Suddenly Kenny realized what was wrong. Yolanda was not emotionally engaged with him and never had been. She kept Kenny at a distance, even while playing a romantic game. The more he thought about it the angrier he got at how little respect she showed him.

Then, suddenly, the feeling shifted. He realized how hurt he was that this woman he cared about refused to take him seriously. It made him very sad.

It is painful to face bruised feelings of sadness. Understanding anger as a cover for sadness is powerful: it reveals the emotion behind the emotion and allows us to uncover the source of the feeling.

Even once we recognize anger as a cover for sadness, we will still get angry at times. But we will have a new way to defuse the anger more quickly. Instead of feeling victimized, we can know that the upset comes from some kind of loss. This is neither self-indulgent nor sentimental. It is a more effective way to see the larger picture and a key to getting ourselves back on track.

> When we see anger as a temporary response to pain and loss, it will lose some of its urgency.

When we understand that what really matters is emotional health and balance, rather than finding the right person or thing to blame, we should be able to begin to move past angry feelings more dependably. Anger will have less power over us, and we won't feel so out of control. When we see anger as a temporary response to pain and loss, it will lose some of its urgency. We may even find ourselves becoming angry less often.

Emotional healing starts from the inside. Healing enhances our power to generate and manage our lives as we choose. Blaming gives that power away. We may still get angry. We don't have to stay there.

Try this: Recall something that happened recently that made you angry. Who or what did it to you? Now look for the loss under the angry feeling: a loss of time, money, self-esteem or something else you value. The quicker you can recognize the loss instead of focusing on the perpetrator, the faster you'll be able to move past anger and back to a state of balance.

Summary

- Anger is an emotional response to feeling victimized.
- Anger that can be explosive distorts normal thinking.
- Habits and childhood learning influence how individuals deal with feelings of anger.
- Hatred is self-sustaining, frozen anger.
- Underneath the violation of anger is sadness associated with some kind of loss.

CHAPTER 13

Fear and Excitement

Fear is a powerful and ancient emotion. From its origins as a life-saving force, fear preserves life by alerting us to danger.

In the Circle of Emotion, fear is unique in important ways. Fear is about the future rather than the past or present. Unlike love, happiness, sadness and anger, which are responses to what has already happened, fear is about what might happen next. Fear always involves an element of the unknown. It can be so strong that it takes over the emotional system entirely, overwhelming all

> Fear preserves life by alerting us to danger.

other kinds of feelings. It is a powerful motivator with a sense of urgency linked to the primal struggle for survival.

Fear is indispensable to our well-being when it steers us away from danger and guides us toward safety. It can become a problem when it gets out of control and hijacks our ability to think clearly, especially when not justified by real danger.

Powerful fear

Powerful fear is immediate. It commands our attention. The more afraid we are, the less we are able to feel or think of anything else.

When our awareness registers a threat to life or something we value, we respond instantly. We stop what we are doing and focus on the threat quietly so as to learn as much as possible without attracting attention. Breathing becomes shallower. Adrenaline rushes into the bloodstream increasing our heart rate. Blood flows to the extremities and away from internal processes such as digestion. These physiological changes prepare us to do whatever is necessary to save ourselves in a potentially life-threatening crisis.

> "A good scare is worth more to a man than good advice."
> – EDWIN WATSON HOWE, magazine editor

Fear takes over our minds as well as our bodies. Thinking sharpens: *What is this threat? How dangerous is it? What do I know from previous life experiences about what's likely to happen and how should I respond? Do I run, fight, scream, or what?* When fear commands our attention, other kinds of feelings vanish.

The automatic response to fear is consistent across many species. From its primal origins, fear became woven into the human emotional system as a full-blown emotion. What was once a mechanical life-preserving reaction in lower species became a powerful emotional state in people.

A future orientation

Fear anticipates potential loss. Even if we are not threatened physically, something we value feels at risk. The feeling can be sharp and dramatic: a speeding car screeches around a corner and you jump out of the way. Or it can be more subtle and feel like worry. If your elderly aunt does not answer the phone when you call, you might be concerned that something happened to her. Each time, fear arises in response to something we imagine could happen in the near or longer term future that we don't want to happen.

What if you woke up one morning with a mysterious abdominal pain. It hurt when you sat up in bed. You wonder what it means.

Perhaps you'd review what you had for dinner the previous night. Temporary indigestion would not be so bad, but what if it gets worse? It might occur to you that this could be the first symptom of a serious disease. Could it be stomach cancer? That would be awful!

If the pain lasts for several days or worsens, you would get more concerned. Eventually you go to the doctor to have it checked out. Fear of a potentially bad future, maybe even something

> "Fear, true fear, is a savage frenzy. Of all the insanities of which we are capable, it is surely the most cruel."
> – GEORGES BERNANOS, novelist

as horrible as stomach cancer, would have gotten you to act to safeguard your health, to maintain or restore Oneness with your personal well-being.

Gut grabbing powerful fear concerns the immediate future—how do I avoid or escape *this* threat *this* instant? All conscious animals including humans feel such fear. But only in people does fear extend beyond momentary danger to more distant imagined perils. A zebra on the plains of Africa is not concerned with lions that might attack tomorrow

> **Fear anticipates potential loss.**

or next year. It is totally occupied with a lion prowling nearby today.

As intelligent animals we recognize patterns and learn to predict what is likely to happen later today, next month, even years from now. Anticipating the future gives us some control over what will happen so we can reduce our fear. When we know in advance, we can take steps to avoid potential danger. Winter will be cold. We prepare to heat our homes in September so as to avoid freezing in January.

The unknown

Fear requires at least an element of the unknown. If we know exactly what is going to happen *and* what it will mean, we do not feel afraid. In the face of the unknown we have to guess. When we are fearful, we imagine undesirable consequences.

Imagine you are out camping in the woods. As you lie down to go to sleep, you hear a rustling sound in the bushes beyond the light of your campfire. Your eyes pop open and you feel afraid. Why? Certainly you are not afraid of the bushes. But bushes moving in the dark means something unknown is out there. It could be a large and dangerous animal. You consider whether these woods are inhabited by bears or mountain lions. Have you heard of a prison break nearby? Your mind does cartwheels about the possible terrors that might befall you... until a raccoon noses into the campfire light, sniffs around, and moves away.

The unknown can be local and limited or vast and vague. Without strong winds, rustling bushes in the dark can only be caused by some kind of animal. The animal has to be bigger than a mouse and could be much larger. You can tell by the sound where the bush is. The unknown you have to solve is limited by specific consider-ations: where is it, what is it, is it a threat, what should I do?

Fear of old age is different. Fear of aging is not about the years but about the unknown consequences of growing old.

> "Fear comes from uncertainty. When we are absolutely certain... we are almost impervious to fear."
> – WILLIAM CONGREVE, playwright

We fear incapacitating illness or mental deterioration. We may be afraid we won't have enough money when we are too old and weak to earn more. We cannot know exactly what will befall us as we age, and that uncertain future may make us afraid.

UNCERTAINTY THAT UNDERMINES HAPPINESS

Harvard professor and happiness researcher Dr. Daniel Gilbert writes that uncertainty about something bad that might happen makes people even more unhappy than knowing for sure that the bad thing will occur. In a study in Holland, subjects who were told they might get painful electric shocks were more fearful and uncomfortable than those told they would definitely get shocked. Dr. Gilbert suggests that knowing something bad will surely happen gives us a chance to make peace with our fate, to sorrow for our losses and move on. Uncertainty is scarier simply because we don't know.

Do you look to your future as filled more with opportunities or with dangers? How we interpret an uncertain future plays a huge part in how afraid we feel when new situations present themselves. Retraining our imagination to anticipate good news in uncertain times can make us less afraid.

During the dark days of World War II, President Franklin Delano Roosevelt told Americans, "The only thing we have to fear is fear itself." His inspirational message was about transcending the fear of the unknown. Roosevelt knew that fear paralyzes people and makes them unable to act. He transformed a nation's fear of the unknown and inspired generations of people to be courageous in the face of an uncertain future.

Understanding what we are afraid of undermines its power over us by diminishing the element of the unknown. Film director Alfred Hitchcock, who was famous for making scary movies, said, "The only way to get rid of my fears is to make films about them."

Fear by association

We learn to associate similar phenomena. When we encounter something new that resembles something we already know, we naturally associate the new thing with what we know, or believe we know, about the old one. Once you have been stung by a bee and you know how much it hurts, you will avoid hornets and wasps. This is normal, healthy learning that serves self preservation. But it can also make us feel fear that is completely unwarranted.

Fernando had been in an earthquake once back home in Chile. The trembling ground and swaying buildings terrified him so badly that he could not sleep properly for weeks. Even years later when a heavy truck rumbled by or a low-flying aircraft rattled his windows, his heart leapt to his throat. He knew he was not in danger, but he could not easily control the feeling. The terror of the day the earth moved beneath his feet had upset him so deeply.

Fear by association can lead to unnecessary suffering when we become afraid of something harmless that reminds us of past danger. We have to learn to distinguish current threats from old associations. The five steps below can help us retrain ourselves against this kind of unwarranted fear.

Worry

Do you worry a lot? Worry is a kind of fear that has become disengaged from the authentic root of fear: preserving life and safety. It is primarily a mental activity, "thinking afraid" rather than feeling afraid. Worry has a spinning quality of thought. It can become a consuming inner monologue without the normal body sensations associated with fear.

> "Worry is the misuse of imagination."
> – DAN ZADRA, author

People who worry dwell on imagined future bad consequences without evaluating their likelihood and implications. Typically, they think about what can go wrong over and over without taking steps to address their concern. Worry does not accomplish anything useful; it simply torments the mind.

It is essential to distinguish legitimate feelings of fear that inspire some useful response from the habit of worry, which doesn't. This is important, because we often use the two words interchangeably.

When Harry and Marlene's renegade daughter was 15, she often did not come home when she was supposed to. Occasionally she stayed out all night. They imagined she could be in real trouble or drinking and drugging with unreliable friends. Harry and Marlene said they were worried about her, but actually they were afraid for her safety, and trying whatever they could think of to get her to change. In the same way, a woman who discovers a lump in her breast will tell her friends she is worried when actually she is viscerally afraid of having cancer, and probably taking steps to find out for sure.

Worry happens when a train of thinking loses touch with the feelings that spawned it and takes on a life of its own. Worriers rarely take action to address their concerns; they simply continue to fret over them. Typically, some people worry about lots of things and others hardly ever worry at all. Worry is a rotten habit that hijacks attention and amplifies stress.

My grandmother was a habitual worrier. Whenever we visited her she told us about whatever she was worried about that day. She would talk about a relative who was ill or tell us a bad story from the news. She was simply in the habit of worrying to occupy her mind. Telling her not to worry was pointless because her habit was so deeply ingrained. In her later years our family learned to assess how she was doing by what she was worrying about. If it was about the personal problems of some movie actress and not her own health issues we knew she was having a good day.

Some worriers have built worry into the way they motivate themselves. They are in the habit of creating a mental image of bad consequences to goad themselves into action.

Cassie was worried that she would forget to send her sister-in-law a birthday card. Rather than simply buy and send the card, she imagined how hurt her sister-in-law would feel if Cassie forgot her birthday. Cassie's worry thoughts grew and grew: "She'll hate me if I forget." "She always remembers my birthday." "My brother will be unhappy with me if I'm not nice to his wife." And so on.

The more Cassie thought about it, the more anxious she became. She could feel the tension. Eventually she bought and sent the card. It gave her a great sense of relief.

If you can only pay the rent on time by imagining being evicted if you don't, you are a motivation worrier. If the only way you get yourself to appointments on time is by picturing a disaster should you be late, you are using worry and fear to manipulate yourself into doing something you do not trust yourself to do otherwise.

You *can* pay the rent on time just because it is due. You *can* get to appointments promptly most of the time by arranging your schedule.

Motivational worry is a bad habit rooted in mistrust. As with all ingrained habits it happens automatically. Like all habits, it can't be simply eliminated. But you can start to replace it with other, more effective habits.

It helps to step back from worrying and observe it as if it afflicted someone else. By separating thought from emotion, a worry habit's control over our mind weakens. It's something we have, not something we are.

> "I don't get upset over things I can control, because if I can control them there's no sense in getting upset. And I don't get upset over things I can't control, because if I can't control them there's no sense in getting upset."
> – MICKEY RIVERS, baseball player

Plan ahead of time how you prefer to act so you'll be prepared when the worry voice starts yammering at you.

The worry wall

The "worry wall" is a wall in time. It's the future moment we can't think beyond, when our worst fears will be realized. . When worry takes over your mind, free yourself by imagining past the worry wall.

Hillary had a picnic with friends planned for Sunday. By Friday the forecast predicted rain, and she started to worry. By Saturday heavy rain appeared likely and the worry grew. Hillary imagined herself staring out the window at the mud and rain. She could

183

almost hear the sounds of cranky children fighting indoors, unable to go out to play. She worried about what to do with all the food and wondered when she might get another chance to see her friends.

That dreary, imagined moment when everything goes wrong is the worry wall. Hillary's thinking hit that wall by going no further than the moment of worst consequences on that rainy Sunday.

But what about Monday? Hillary will get up Monday morning and go about her business. She and her family will probably have eaten some of the food at home and put the picnic supplies away for another time. Perhaps they will have gone to the movies. Life will go on. The loss of the picnic will soon be forgotten. The worry will have gained her nothing.

We can go beyond the worry wall by imagining what is likely to happen *after* the moment we are so worried about. It takes looking further into the future and using our good imagination to overcome our bad imagination. The world does not stop at some worried-about event, and neither should our thinking. The more we look beyond the worry wall to what's likely to happen afterward, and then after that, the easier it will be for us to replace the worry habit with the habit of being open to what the future has to offer.

Processing fear

Legitimate fear is essential. Unwarranted fear is a burden. We need to have a way to distinguish one from the other. One strategy is composed of five steps:

First, notice that you feel afraid. This sounds obvious but can be difficult sometimes. Recall that fear makes people turn attention outward. When we are afraid—or scared, nervous, anxious, worried, or panicked—we tend not to notice what's going on inside. Many people do not like to admit to feeling afraid. We may have to train ourselves to observe that we are in fact feeling fearful.

Second, answer the question, "What *exactly* am I afraid of?" You may have to dig deep to find out. Are you afraid of failing or being rejected? Do you fear for the safety of people you love? The first answer that comes to mind might not be the true one. It may require asking

> Answer the question "What exactly am I afraid of?"

the question again and again to find the true source of the fear, some kind of anticipated loss. Recall that fear is always about something unknown in the future. Look for both the "what" and the "when".

Third, determine how likely is it that the bad result will actually happen, and what it would mean if it did. Make yourself step back from the feeling long enough to judge fairly. Or ask for help, especially from someone who knows better.

Sometimes it is impossible to determine how severe the risk is. But examining the legitimacy of our fear sheds light on a dark place in the worry mind. More important, asking the question invokes the calming influence of reason. At the same time, our emotional system will begin to do what it is designed to do: restore balance. If the fear is legitimate, we will be better prepared to address whatever is causing it. If not, we will be calmer for discovering the truth.

Fourth, ask ourselves: "How do we want this to turn out?" Don't assume that the answer is obvious; we must ask explicitly what outcome we desire and stay with it until we have an answer.

Fifth, take action on what we've learned. *Do something.* Even if it's small, taking action puts us more in control of our destiny. We feel less fearful when we reclaim control of the situation by taking action at times when we feel afraid.

This five-step process won't eliminate legitimate fear. But it will reduce the helpless feeling of being trapped in those situations where fear is not merited by real danger.

> "I have not ceased being fearful, but I have ceased to let fear control me."
> – ERICA JONG, novelist

Try this method on something small first, to see how it works. How else could you apply this kind of step-by-step approach? Imagine how different our lives would be if our choices and decisions were based on what we love rather than on what we fear.

Beyond feeling afraid

It is one thing to conquer fear of some unwanted consequence. It's quite another to transcend our fear and take bold action even when we are scared. Since fear evolved to protect us from danger, what moves people to face severe risk in the service of something greater?

The answer is love. Only love transcends fear. Powerful love—as courage—is the extraordinary ability to disregard fearful feelings because something or someone we love is more important, and to take action in spite of our fear.

Courage is what makes a child stand up to the schoolyard bully in the name of justice. It's what makes the whistleblower risk her job to reveal a boss who cheats on the numbers. Courage is what defined Lincoln, Gandhi, and Mandela as some of the most admired figures in history.

Courage is not a feeling. It is not part of the emotional system and does not appear in the Circle of Emotions. It is an act of choice grounded in feelings of Oneness. Life will surely give each of us many opportunities to act courageously as we face risks of various kinds. Each time we get to choose whether love or fear will prevail. Courage transforms ordinary people into heroes and calls forth the heroic in the rest of us.

> "Courage is never letting your actions be influenced by your fears."
> – ARTHUR KOESTLER, author

Excitement

Fear has a unique counterpart in excitement. Excitement generates the same physical and mental responses as fear: the pounding heartbeat, heightened focus and orientation to the future. The difference is that excitement anticipates a good rather than a bad outcome.

Millions of Americans love professional wrestling. They feel a thrill as giant, angry-looking men bellow and threaten to dismember each other. No matter that the matches are carefully choreographed, fans feel a visceral excitement as wrestlers throw each other across the ring.

Were one of these behemoths to threaten you or me under any other circumstances, we would be terrified. Only the certainty that this is entertainment, and that no harm will befall us, allows us to respond to professional wrestling with excitement rather than abject terror.

Fear and excitement are two sides of the same coin. They share physical sensations caused by the compelling power of adrenaline, the chemical that prepares us to fight or run for our lives. The surge of adrenaline in our blood creates a rush that many people find pleasurable. Excitement gives us the adrenaline rush without the prospect of danger. It makes us feel engaged and alive and makes moments feel important.

Advertising messages are created to artificially foster excitement. Through quick-cutting video, loud sound and bright colors advertisers attempt to trick us into feeling excited as we might for something we genuinely care about. Excitement is also key to the success of amusement parks, race tracks and most sports events. People love feeling scared on a fast roller coaster because they know it is mock fear and they are safe. If the risk is real, nobody gets on the ride.

Most of us are easy targets for media-driven messages that life is too dull and should be more exciting. The powerful feeling of the adrenaline rush, which evolved to protect us, makes us vulnerable to the seductive promise of more and more excitement.

It is possible to become hooked on excitement and addicted to the rush of adrenaline. Adrenaline addiction occurs when the *intensity* of life becomes more important than the *quality* of life.* Excitement feels terrific in part because the thrill is temporary. Since the excited feeling lasts only as long as the chemical is in the bloodstream, an adrenaline addict needs continual stimulation to regenerate that feeling.

> The powerful feeling of the adrenaline rush, which evolved to protect us, makes us vulnerable to the seductive promise of more and more excitement.

*see www.adrenalineaddicts.org, Larry I. Meadows

Try this: Next time you notice yourself feeling worried or afraid, ask yourself what you are really afraid of. What's the nature of the loss that could happen? What's the element of the unknown? Can you learn enough about that to make it less fearful?

Summary

- Fear is a primitive emotion that evolved to save us from danger.
- Fear is oriented toward the future and involves an element of the unknown.
- People easily develop habits of fear and worry that do not reflect real danger.
- Excitement is mock fear: it feels physically the same but anticipates a positive outcome.

CHAPTER 14

Fluid Feelings

Most of the time, the way we feel in this moment, or the next, does not fit into neat categories of emotion. Feelings are fluid. Our feelings change continually in response to people, events and internal processes.

Each new moment is unique. While the range of our emotional landscape is familiar, moment to moment details are unpredictable. We travel the territory prepared for the general direction of our journey but not knowing exactly what will come next.

> We travel the emotional territory prepared for the general direction of our journey but not knowing exactly what will come next.

Mixed feelings

The primary emotions in the Circle of Emotions sometimes occur in a pure state. Often, however, our feelings are nuanced and may include a mixture of several kinds of feelings.

Monica's daughter Morgan endured a long and painful battle with leukemia as a child. For many months Morgan's young life hung in the balance. As any parent would, Monica devoted herself relentlessly to Morgan's care, and eventually the disease was cured.

All through Morgan's growing up, Monica was especially protective of her as a result of all they had gone through together. The day Morgan left home to go to college was both a wonderfully happy and a painfully sad day for her mom. Monica was thrilled that her daughter would get to enjoy the future that was once in such doubt. At the same time, her years of raising the daughter who had given her life such meaning were over. Monica cried tears of joy and tears of sadness at the same time.

Mixed feelings can be confusing. It is difficult to know how to respond when pulled in two directions at once. It's even harder when one set of feelings seems to make sense and the other doesn't. Rarely are mixed feelings as easy to understand as Monica's.

> As our emotional system gets healthier, we become more patient with mixed emotions and more confident that the confusion will soon resolve itself.

Feelings can change rapidly. Contrasting emotions sometimes jumble together faster than we can recognize them since feeling follows our wandering attention. The resulting emotional uncertainty can be uncomfortable and difficult to sort out.

In times of confusing emotions, it helps to step back and calm ourselves. Take your time before making key decisions. As our emotional system gets healthier, we become more patient with mixed emotions and more confident that the confusion will soon resolve itself.

Social animals, social emotions

In addition to the primary emotions, we experience a variety of social emotions that arise in response to the almost infinite possibilities of human social interaction. Unlike happiness or fear, feelings such as shame, jealousy or admiration occur only in relation to other people. While each of the social emotions has its own unique flavor, they all operate to support and regulate the workings of human social behavior.

Like most teenagers, 17-year old Angelo enjoyed nothing more than hanging out with his friends. On weekends he and his buddies would get together to talk, laugh, and look for girls. One night they found some beer and took it into the woods to drink. Angelo had too much. He got sick and his friends had to take him home to face the wrath of his parents.

All the next week Angelo's friends wouldn't talk to him. They blamed him for getting them all in trouble. Angelo felt ashamed. He quickly learned the dangers of too much alcohol, not because he got drunk or was punished by his parents, but because of being ostracized by his friends.

Social emotions stabilize communities by reinforcing behavior that makes the community stronger. Feelings of pride, gratitude and empathy strengthen social bonds that bring people together. Embarrassment and guilt, on the other hand, deter us from repeating certain actions by making us feel badly for having done them.

Social emotions that correspond to the Oneness side of the Circle of Emotion include gratitude, admiration, pride, sympathy, empathy, and compassion. Each of these connects a person with others. Gratitude and admiration bring us closer to those whom we respect and appreciate. Empathy helps us imagine what it would be like to live in someone else's shoes. Pride—the pride we feel for our children for their accomplishments—affirms bonds of personal relationships.

> "If you want others to be happy, practice compassion. If you want to be happy, practice compassion."
> – THE DALAI LAMA

On the other side of the Circle of Emotion are contempt and jealousy, social variations on anger. Shyness is a kind of fear, the fear of social inadequacy. Social emotions linked to sadness include guilt: we feel badly about our perceived failures. Envy is a sad emotion (we lack what we wish we had) as is shame. Sympathy is a mix of compassion, a Oneness emotion, and sadness on someone else's behalf.

The social emotions exist to benefit interpersonal relationships and strengthen social bonds. They show up in more subtle varieties than we can name. Uncomfortable social feelings indicate something is off: we need to correct a situation or learn from it. Rewarding social emotions, such as gratitude or empathy, deepen bonds of connection and enrich our lives.

Insecurity and "cool"

Social insecurity affects virtually everybody at some time or other. Insecurity is a form of fear: the fear of failing, looking bad or not measuring up. Insecurity and low self-esteem occur when we compare ourselves unfavorably to others or to an image of how we think we should be. Even one who is confident in one area of life can feel painfully insecure in another.

Insecurity makes fluid feelings stop, for the moment, as we become sharply aware of our perceived inadequacy. Confidence and clarity shut down. Insecurity is especially recognizable in young people.

Seanna and her friends all dress exactly alike. They wear their hair the same way, listen to the same music and carry the same kinds of cell phones. None of them dares stray from the strict conformity that makes them the "in" group at their high school.

Seanna refuses to put on a warm coat on cold winter mornings because her friends don't. It is more important to her to be stylish in an open pea coat, even though she is freezing cold. The only way she feels secure is by clinging to the strict demands of her peer group.

I often do and say dumb things when I am feeling insecure, and you probably do too. We may not even be aware of the feeling until the embarrassing words have left our mouths. When people act in odd ways that seem awkward or out of character, it's often because they are feeling insecure.

Tony and Jack sit near each other at hockey games. They have had season tickets for years. Jack is clever and funny; Tony is not. Jack makes frequent wisecracks and jokes that entertain their section of the arena. Tony's attempts at humor seem lame by comparison.

Occasionally Tony will repeat a joke in the third period that Jack had made in the first period of the same game. Tony wants to be funny like Jack, and feels insecure that he's not. Nobody laughs at Tony's retelling of the joke, which makes him feel even worse.

Insecurity is a problem without an easy solution because it's so hard to change your attitude from within that point of view: you can't convince yourself to feel successful from the viewpoint of "I'm a failure." If you struggle with the painful feeling of insecurity, remember that the feelings is temporary. If you are worried what other people might be thinking about you, it may help to recall that they are probably not thinking about you at all, but worried about what *you* might be thinking about *them*.

As we grow emotionally healthier and more confident, our insecurities will naturally diminish but may never disappear. The only thing to do in a moment of painful insecurity is to recognize what is happening, forgive ourselves for being human, and move on. Feelings are fluid and will change in the next moment, as our attention turns to whatever comes next.

Beware of a common social response to feeling insecure, the desire to act "cool," in the sense of disengaging emotionally. The impulse to put on a "cool" act stems from the desire to protect ourselves from hurt by pretending not to care. Unfortunately, the cost of creating social distance is usually greater than the benefit. Acting "cool" in this way shuts down opportunities to connect. It is not a helpful strategy for a more satisfying life. People who strive to be "cool," and actually succeed in learning to squelch their feelings, find it very difficult to unlearn.

HUMOR

Humor is not an emotion, yet the appreciation of humor is one of the most consistent and treasured emotional responses we have. We love finding things funny and we love to laugh. Smiling and laughing in response to humor generates a strong Oneness feeling—a feeling of sharing in the human condition.

Recognition of humor—getting the joke—is a cognitive process that leads to an emotional response. It happens when previously incongruous elements come together in a particular unexpected way. Rod A. Martin, in his book *The Psychology of Humor* (2007), considers humorous interaction a form of play. In Arthur Koestler's *The Act of Creation* (1964), humor is presented as one of three important areas of creativity (along with art and science). Koestler argues that humor emerges under certain social conditions when a given event is simultaneously perceived from two normally unrelated frames of reference.

Appreciation of humor is highly social: we share laughter with others much more than we laugh alone. When laughing and smiling with other people, we naturally feel closer to them. A humorous remark made to defuse nervousness is a good example of using humor to enhance feelings of Oneness.

People who are funny tend to be popular, and a good sense of humor is one of the chief traits single people list as desirable in a potential mate. Laughing and smiling contributes to a feeling of good health and a sense of well-being. Cheerfulness and a ready appreciation of humor is often a good indicator of emotional health as well.

Patterns of emotion

As a child Dana was irrepressible. She was full of energy and confidence, fearlessly climbing trees and racing her bicycle down hills. Her mother tried to explain why Dana should be more careful, but nothing she said made a difference. Until she discovered guilt.

While it did not help to warn her daughter that she could be badly hurt, telling Dana how badly her parents would feel if Dana hurt herself worked beautifully. Dana slowed down. Whenever she felt the impulse to go fast, she thought of how her parents would feel should anything bad happen. Guilt worked perfectly, but at a cost.

As an adult, Dana feels guilty frequently. She feels guilty about not cooking dinner for her husband though he prefers to do the cooking himself. When facing a task she might not feel like doing, she uses guilt to manipulate herself

"For good and evil, man is a free creative spirit. This produces the very queer world we live in, a world in continuous creation and therefore continuous change and insecurity."
– JOYCE CARY, novelist

into action. And when she cannot control the risky behavior of her own daughter, she turns to the time-honored guilt trip to coerce her daughter into compliance.

Guilt for Dana became linked to motivation when her parents used guilt to get her to behave. Originally employed to motivate her to be careful, it blossomed into a universal motivator that she unconsciously applies to much of what she does. It's a burden, to be sure, but it works.

Patterns of emotion, such as some of the habits discussed in previous chapters, establish themselves early on. Often a single incident in childhood generates a response that grows into a lifelong pattern. Some people, like Dana, feel guilty all the time. Others might be chronically envious or ashamed.

Overcoming lifelong patterns of emotion is difficult but not impossible. It may help to trace them back to their origins. But even understanding how these complex patterns came to be offers no guarantee that we will ever be free of them. Remember that these dysfunctional patterns are not inseparable parts of us: they are tendencies we developed over time and behaviors we repeat. Once upon a time they came into being for a reason, even if that reason is no longer valid.

Occasionally people are able to simply drop old, useless patterns and walk away from them. More often, the best we can do is make peace with them. In time, by using each recurrence as an opportunity to make different choices, we may be able to slowly let them dissolve.

At the other end of the spectrum, it is possible to cultivate patterns of life-affirming emotion. Noticing the love and satisfaction we have in our lives reinforces those good feelings. Developing an attitude of grateful appreciation generates a pattern of being thankful for, and content with, the many wonderful parts of life.

Since feeling follows attention, we can pursue feeling better more of the time by remembering to put attention on what we love and enjoy instead of the parts we dislike. Tough times will still be there. But the more we focus our attention on the pleasurable aspects of our lives, the more we cause our fluid emotions to flow toward the healthy, happy Oneness feelings we cherish.

> Since feeling follows attention, we can pursue feeling better by remembering to put attention on what we love and enjoy.

Try this: Imagine you were advising a younger person about some kind of insecurity. You'd probably tell that person that his or her perceived problem was only a perception, and not significant compared to positive traits and abilities. Then turn the advice around on yourself.

Summary

- We often feel a mixture of different kinds of feelings.
- Social emotions arise from and regulate interpersonal relations.
- Everyone feels social insecurity sometimes.

CHAPTER 15

Self Love

Walking among the Himalayan Mountains is unnerving. The grandeur and sheer magnificence of the landscape is overwhelming. The complete absence of the sound of machinery creates a peacefulness almost beyond imagining.

At the same time, the scale is disorienting. You lose track of normal indicators of size and distance. At home, we are familiar with the size of common objects such as trees, cars and buildings. In the vast landscape of the Himalayas the spaces and shapes are so huge that you see a mountain ahead of you and cannot tell if it is two miles away or twenty. You are unable to judge if it rises a few hundred feet or several thousand. It makes you feel small.

After trekking for days in the Khumbu region of Nepal, the area around Mount Everest, I started to feel terribly insignificant. The towering Himalayas rose like mighty kings around me and I felt puny. It got worse as the days passed.

Settled into camp at about 16,000 feet near a summer grazing valley called Dingboche, we were two days short of our destination, the base of Mount Everest. I wandered off alone from the tents of our trekking group to see what I could find. The air smelled incredibly crisp and pure.

A large yak stood among the low scrub plants in a pen surrounded by stone walls. There were no trees. The only person I saw was a woman with a big sack on her back. She was picking up clumps of dried yak dung to use as fuel for her cooking fire.

I climbed a hill on the lower flank of Lhotse, the world's fourth highest mountain, sat on a big rock and looked out over the valley. Then I looked up and saw an extraordinary sight. Huge fluted walls of ice gleamed in the afternoon sun. The spectacular Chukhung glacier stretched across an indeterminate span and rose to an unknowable height in the crystal mountain sky.

The beauty of this massive glacier struck me like a visual symphony. I was overwhelmed. Tears filled my eyes, as they do now as I write this. I sat on the rock and gazed on as magnificent a sight as I have ever seen. I imagined that the glacier had stood in its regal splendor for thousands, perhaps hundreds of thousands of years, and would still be there thousands of years after my meager decades on earth were past. Compared to these mountains and glaciers I was a mere speck.

I don't know how long I sat there, feeling utterly insignificant. I shifted my weight on the hard rock. Suddenly, my perspective turned completely upside down. I smiled. I looked down at my hands and flexed my fingers. I turned to the glacier and said, "You can't move like that." The thought made me laugh. I thought of all the things I've done and the places I've been while that big old glacier was stuck on the side of a mountain. I looked around at the other great mountains, Lhotse behind me and Cholatse to my right. None of them could budge. Not one of them could feel what I felt, or think, or love. Great as they were as mountains, they were just big hunks of rock and ice, fixed in one place forever, silent sentinels doing nothing.

It was an exhilarating realization. By the time I left my rock and returned to camp, I knew that these great mountains had their noble place in this world. And so did I. I am unique and as valid

> There is a place on this earth for every one of us, and each of us merits dignity and respect simply for being here.

in my way as the Himalayas are in theirs. By inevitable extension, everyone and everything else is too.

There is a place on this earth for every one of us, and each of us merits dignity and respect simply for being here. I may be smarter than some people, not as tall as others, older or younger. I am unique, and so are you. My value as a human being is independent of yours. My essential dignity is not less than that of presidents nor more than that of the homeless on the streets. I am not less or more worthy of existence than Mount Everest.

That December day in the Himalayas taught me about self love.

Two days later I stood atop an 18,200-foot hill called Kala Pattar and watched the golden sunset light creep up the western face of Everest. No longer did I feel less worthy than the landscape I had the immense good fortune to visit. Everest had its attributes; I had mine.

We coexisted as partners with everyone and everything else in the greater scheme of it all.

Self love is simply being at One with yourself. On a feeling level, self love is about acceptance rather than attraction, a sense of wholeness and completeness without limit or qualification. As with the love of another person, the feeling of self love is impossible to describe in words and very difficult to talk about at all. It is entirely an inner experience.

We have looked at the subtleties of the various emotions, but self love has no subtleties or shadings. It is pure Oneness. Though we may be more inclined to accept ourselves as we are at some times than others, self love is not a matter of degree. At any given time you either have it or you don't.

Babies and many young children have this kind of self acceptance for a while. You see it as they play, taking delight in themselves and their bodies. But it is hard to maintain through the confusing years of later childhood and adolescence when rapid changes and new pressures take their toll. In adulthood, self acceptance is something we have to grow into, as we learn to be at peace with the complex person we have become.

> Self love is simply being at One with yourself.

Self love does not generate strong feelings. It does not make us feel happy, wistful, or tender. Unlike the emotional states that fill us up, self love empties us out. It replaces self hatred, guilt, anger, disappointment and fear with openness and a quality of freedom. It is quite a wonderful sensation.

You don't know what you don't know until you know it. You can't know what it is like to accept yourself as you are until you do. Accepting yourself as you are means you never have to feel stuck with your personality or your looks. On the contrary, self acceptance frees you to grow and become more the way you might like to be. When you accept yourself wholly and without judgment you have access to all your mental, emotional and spiritual resources to move forward.

Imagine for a moment that you—your character and your life—are a perfect work in progress. You are not the final version of yourself, more like a draft version a writer creates before editing and refining. There may be much you want to change. But for the moment, imagine you are where you are supposed to be.

From this vantage point you can see your past without guilt or prejudice. Whatever path you took to get to today is behind you. The characteristics you see as defects or flaws you came by honestly. The bad habits got started for good reasons at the time even if they have now outlived their usefulness.

> "The greatest success is successful self-acceptance."
> – BEN SWEET, author

Your weaknesses and ignorance present opportunities to develop and learn. The mistakes you made were just mistakes.

What a terrific place to be: right here, right now.

Looking at life this way does not mean your life is uniformly excellent or that you have arrived exactly where you eventually want to be. Even those who are the healthiest emotionally are keenly aware of their faults. They care about improving themselves and developing better habits. What they have learned, though, is that the future starts only right now. Whatever you did in the past that you regret is over. It need not deter you from moving forward unless you let it. Self love is a quiet place unpolluted by all the "should haves" and "could haves" most of us put up with all the time.

When my daughters were young we used to say around our house that the only thing to do with a mistake is to fix it. When you accept yourself, you are more likely to start fixing mistakes and less likely to dwell on what they might mean about you. They don't mean anything, unless you let them.

There is no trick to developing self love. An attitude of kindness and compassion opens the door. You move forward by taking action consistent with what you want the future to include. If you ask yourself what the person you want to become—your ideal future self—would do each time you face a difficult choice, an answer will appear. If you act in line with that answer you move yourself closer to becoming that person.

> Self love is a quiet place unpolluted by all the "should haves" and "could haves" most of us put up with all the time.

The remarkable thing about self love is the way it opens you to love others. Genuine self love is not egotistical because it steers attention away from yourself. By contrast, people who seem stuck on how wonderful they are, and need reinforcement from others, are simply insecure.

Self love is a foundation: the ability to love other people emanates from the ability to love yourself. The same principle of acceptance applies. Oneness starts from within. That's where you come from and who you are: one being. You have to accept your own self as a starting point before you can fully share yourself with another person. Otherwise, you would have nothing to share.

Self love is easy to spot in other people. It looks like confidence, relaxation, enthusiasm, calm or cheerfulness. Contrast that to emotionally needy people who demand too much attention, constantly asking others to validate them because they feel so unsure of themselves.

Actually, though, all of us are a mix: sometimes we feel confident, sometimes insecure. Sometimes we accept ourselves as we are, at other times we think only of our faults and failures. As we get older, the balance usually shifts in a positive direction as we make peace with ourselves and the contents of our lives.

> "Acceptance is the truest kinship with humanity."
> – G. K. CHESTERTON, philosopher

Learning to love yourself is not complicated. In principle, it is astonishingly simple. You will not find self love discussed much in public because it is so basic and so abstract. Your friends won't talk about it because there is so little to say.

Honest, compassionate self-examination prepares you for self love. Intimate moments with close family and dear friends reveal it. Quiet walks in Nature, good books and the presence of great art inspire it. Only you will know when you feel it.

THE MIRROR EXERCISE

During a discouraging period in my life when I felt aimless and lost, I made up a routine that dramatically changed my inner relationship. Every night I went into the bathroom, looked at myself in the mirror, and in the privacy behind a closed door said out loud: **"I appreciate you. I respect you. I love you."** Even if I had already gone to bed, I forced myself up and into the bathroom to repeat this with as much sincerity as I could muster. On bad days it was difficult and felt like a lie, but I did it anyway.

After about half a year of doing this faithfully, I noticed that something was different. My level of self acceptance had shifted for the better. How much it was due to the nightly drill at the mirror I can't say for sure. But my inner relationship had changed permanently. I am still painfully aware of my shortcomings and there are days when I feel like a failure. But deep down I know that life is not pointless and my place on earth is as valid as anyone else's.

You are a unified being. All the elements of your physical body, spirit, mind and feelings add up to just one you. Oneness is where you come from. Self love is rediscovering that Oneness and accepting it. It is coming home to where you have always been.

Try this: Whatever happens today, accept yourself exactly as you are, at least for the moment. You don't have to be proud of everything you've done; you might prefer to act differently the next time. Just accept what you've done for the moment without judgment. Notice how acceptance helps you to move on.

Summary

- Self love is the foundation for loving others.
- The present moment is a temporary step in our continuing development and growth.
- Self-acceptance is the key to self love.

Mt. Everest

BIBLIOGRAPHY

Bradberry, Travis and Greaves, Jean, **Emotional Intelligence 2.0**, TalentSmart, 2009 *A handbook of strategies to increase emotional Intelligence.*

Borysenko, Joan, **The Power of the Mind to Heal**, Hay House, 1995 *A blend of medicine, spirituality and alternative healing practices to treat physical and emotional ailments.*

Borysenko, Joan, **Minding the Body, Mending the Mind,** Da Capo Press, 2007 *A guide to self healing.*

Damasio, Antonio, **Looking for Spinoza: Joy, Sorrow and the Feeling Brain**. Harcourt, 2003. *A neurologist's examination of the body processes that underlie emotion.*

Damasio, Antonio, **Descartes' Error: Emotion, Reason, and the Human Brain**, Harper, 1995 *A discussion of the role of emotions in decision making.*

Gilbert, Daniel, **Stumbling on Happiness**, Vintage, 2007 *The limitations of our imagination get in the way of pursuing real happiness.*

Gladwell, Malcolm. **The Tipping Point**, Little Brown & Co., 2000. *How small ideas and events can trigger major changes.*

Gottman, John, **Raising an Emotionally Intelligent Child,,** Simon & Shuster, 1998. *Helping children to be more emotionally aware and apply their feeling life to a variety of life situations.*

Frankl, Viktor, **Man's Search for Meaning** *A psychiatrist's lessons from his time in a Nazi concentration camp.*

Fritz, Robert, **The Path of Least Resistance**, Ballantine Books, 1989. *Recognizing the structure underlying human behavior and using it to create what you want.*

Fritz, Robert, **Your Life as Art,** Newfane Press, 2002 *Using the techniques artists use in creating art to make up your life.*

Horwitz, Allan & Wakefield, Jerome. **The Loss of Sadness: How Psychiatry Transformed Normal Sorrow into Depressive Disorder,** Oxford U. Press, 2007 *Stepping back from the medicalization of ordinary, if uncomfortable, life passages.*

Hrdy, Sarah, **Mothers and Others: The Evolutionary Origins of Mutual Understanding,** Harvard U. Press, 2009 *How humans evolved as a cooperative species through a different style of mothering.*

Koestler, Arthur, **The Act of Creation**, 1964 *An early discussion of the nature of the creative process.*

Nussbaum, Martha C., **Upheavals of Thought: the Intelligence of Emotions.** Cambridge U. Press, 2001 *An academic discussion of the role emotions play in regulating behavior.*

Tart, Charles, **Waking Up, Overcoming the Obstacles to Human Potential**, New Science Library, 1986. *A guide to becoming more awake in the world and more spiritually aware.*

Tolle, Echkart, **The Power of Now**, New World Library, 1999. *Spiritual teaching about living in the moment.*

ACKNOWLEDGMENTS:

Thanks to my teachers, too numerous to name. Parents, of course, and those who intentionally or unwittingly helped me learn all that went into this project. Two influential teachers of note are Vincent Scully and Robert Fritz.

Thanks to readers at various stages whose responses helped shape the text: Mary Murphy, Charles Lewis, Pam Fantini, Steve Marantz, Janet Parker, Tod Frueh, and those who could not finish earlier versions.

Thanks to developmental editor Brandon Yusuf Toropov who helped shape the ideas into a coherent whole. Brandon's website is iwordsmith.com. Also designer Jerry Dorris of authorsupport.com.

Thanks to my daughters: Elizabeth who helped me look into the subject of emotions in new ways and Carrie and who tolerated my working on it while not having a regular job. Special thanks to my wife Anne Lucas for her relentless support and love.

Made in the USA
Lexington, KY
31 May 2011